BYGONE ATTRACTIONS OF CHITTENDEN COUNTY

BYGONE ATTRACTIONS OF CHITTENDEN COUNTY

Bob Blanchard

Burlington, VT

Onion River Press
Burlington, VT 05401
www.onionriverpress.com
info@onionriverpress.com

Publisher's Cataloging-in-Publication Data
Names: Blanchard, Bob, author.
Title: Bygone attractions of Chittenden county / Bob Blanchard.
Description: Burlington, VT: Onion River Press, 2024.
Identifiers: LCCN: 2023918833 | ISBN: 978-1-957184-44-9
Subjects: LCSH Chittenden County (Vt.)--History. | Chittenden County (Vt.)--Guidebooks. | Chittenden County (Vt.)--Description and travel. | Vermont--Description and travel. | Vermont--Social life and customs. | Vermont--History. BISAC ARCHITECTURE / Buildings / Landmarks & Monuments | HISTORY / United States / State & Local / New England (CT, MA, ME, NH, RI, VT) | SOCIAL SCIENCE / Customs & Traditions
Classification: LCC F57.C5 .B53 2024 | DDC 917.43/17/0443--dc23

Acknowledgements

Thanks to my editor Rachel Fisher and her staff at the Onion River Press for their great help in putting this book together.

Many thanks to the staff at UVM Silver Special Collections for their patient assistance to me in my many trips to their facility over the course of researching this book. And also thanks to the University of Vermont for making the images at Silver Special Collections readily available to me and to the readers of this book.

Special mention needs to be made of the James Detore photographic archive at UVM. Mr. Detore photographed scenes in the Burlington area from the late 30s to the mid 60s. The majority of the images in this book are photographs that were taken by him.

Thanks also to Janie Merola McKenzie for access to her Uncle Louie Merola's collection of historic photos of Chittenden County.

Also contributing images, information, or both, were Bob Recupero, Richard Crabtree, Elliot Douglas, Sharon Cioffi Joiner, Josephine Bove, the children and grandchildren of Bernie Kriesel, Alfred Holden, Jerry Chase, John Baeder, Dan Higgins, Patrick Seymour of the Theatre Historical Society of America, Kevin Johnson of the Penobscot Marine Museum, Al's French Frys, the Vermont State Archives, the Milton Vermont Historical Society, the National Archives, Vermont Life Magazine, Mary Ellen Hurlbut Farrow, South Burlington Planning and Zoning, and the online archive of the Burlington Free Press via newspapers.com.

Also, as always, thanks to my family, Linda, James, Viki and Luna. Special thanks to my wife Linda for her great patience as I pursue my "obsession" with local history.

This book is dedicated to the memory of our son
John William Blanchard.

Contents

Preface

In a way this book is a follow up to my first book *Lost Burlington, Vermont.* That book chronicled the history of the many historic buildings and other features in Burlington that have been lost. But this volume differs from "Lost Burlington" in several significant ways. The geographic scope is not limited to Burlington, but covers all of Chittenden County. Also, buildings housing the places featured in this book may still be around. It's the businesses themselves that are gone.

Probably the most significant difference is that while *Lost Burlington* was focused on the history of lost landmark structures, this book is more of a nostalgic look at places that would not be considered landmarks. It covers the rise of leisure activity in the culture, and the places in the area where people went to eat, drink, shop, see a movie, bowl, and otherwise have a good time. The structures housing these establishments, with a few exceptions, would hardly be considered iconic. Places like local snack bars, bowling alleys, suburban cinemas and the like were usually housed in unremarkable buildings. There are exceptions of course, but what was important to people were the experiences that they had and the memories they created at these places.

In the past four years I've done a lot of work on local history, and from that experience I've learned that nostalgia is something that far more people relate to than history. People want to hear about and see photos of places that they experienced in their lifetimes. So this book is a nostalgic look back at the many places in Chittenden County that were enjoyed by countless people over the years. Eventually nostalgia will become history as the years go by and the people that experienced the places in this book pass from the scene. So hopefully, in addition to providing a lot of memories for people while they're still around, this book will be a resource to future generations so that they can see the places where their parents and grandparents went for a good time "back in the day."

As the title indicates, the area covered is Chittenden County, Vermont (with one exception). The places covered are all gone, but I did waive that requirement for three iconic eateries that are still going strong as this is being written. Since no one knows what the future holds, I thought it would be a shame not to include them since they go so far back. The time frame covered by the book is the 30s through the 70s. So any place that was in business during those decades is considered eligible to be included in this book.

Since nothing evokes memories like photographs, I've included many. Most are of good or excellent quality, but some places were elusive when it came to getting a good image. So a few images of lower quality are included out of necessity. I've tried to cover as many places as possible, although I'm sure some may be disappointed that they don't find everything they're looking for. The places covered feature a short history along with at least one photograph.

Introduction

The middle portion of the 20th century brought a dizzying array of improvements to American life. Even people born as late as the 50s, like myself, experienced coal burning furnaces at home and ice boxes for refrigeration. But soon, shoveling coal into the basement furnace was replaced by a mere turning of the thermostat on the wall. Semi-weekly visits by the ice man and the drudgery of emptying the drip pan were replaced by an electric refrigerator that kept things cold and even frozen with no effort at all.

Changes like these may not have been as significant as the coming of the railroad and electricity in earlier days. Those were truly life changing, especially the coming of electric light. But refrigeration and automatic furnaces were only two of the many improvements in daily life that started in the early 20th century and continue to this day.

Among other notable improvements in everyday life was the reduction of the number of hours worked and the increasing affluence of the middle class. Taken together, these changes resulted in two new concepts, leisure time and disposable income, which were nearly unknown to earlier generations. Added to that was rising car ownership as manufacturing efficiency drove prices down to levels affordable by increasing numbers of middle class people. These trends really took off in the post World War II years as America enjoyed a prosperity unparalleled in human history. The net effect of all of this was a tremendous increase in the demand for recreational opportunities.

Enterprising business people of all types rose to the occasion, creating a wide array of attractions to accommodate these newly mobile Americans with free time and money to spend. The vacation and the road trip became a standard part of family life starting as early as the 30s, but they really exploded with the post war prosperity of the country and the rise of the car culture.

This book will document in words and photographs the many places in Vermont's Chittenden County that were created as part of that recreational infrastructure that emerged in the 30s, and continued on through the Baby Boom years of the 20th century. Locals on a day trip or tourists spending weeks in the area needed a place to stay, places to eat, and increasingly, entertainment options. As the title suggests, the places covered in this book that provided so much fun and even joy to so many are now gone.

There are many places covered in this book, and there is much more to be said about some than about others. So the mini-histories of each place can run to a couple of pages or be as short as a paragraph or two. I've also taken the liberty of adding a few personal reminiscences here and there to get these memories down on paper while there's still time.

People of a certain age who grew up in the area or went to college here will remember many of the attractions featured in this book. So hopefully the photos and short histories will evoke happy memories for many. For others, I hope that this book will open a window into the past and give you a glimpse of the local spots people enjoyed for decades.

Chittenden County

Chittenden County Vermont is ideally situated for those who enjoy outdoor recreation. Adjacent Lake Champlain, the sixth largest fresh water lake in the country, offers boating, swimming, fishing and camping by its shores, or just sightseeing as you drive along its shoreline. Lake views from towns like Burlington, Shelburne, Colchester and South Burlington are some of the most scenic vistas in the nation. Generations of locals and tourists alike have marveled as they gazed across the wide water to the splendid sight of New York's Adirondack mountains on the far shore. Whether this view is taken in from high above, as from Burlington's Battery Park, or from along the lakefront itself, it is a view not soon forgotten, especially at sunset.

If you turn your gaze in the other direction, to the east rise the Green Mountains, one of the oldest mountain ranges in the country. Their beauty changes with the seasons, from their namesake green in summer, to the blaze of fall, and then snow-capped splendor through Vermont's long winter. The mountains also offer ample options for outdoor enthusiasts, just a short drive from the county's population centers. From skiing to hiking, fly fishing to hunting, or just taking a drive to cool off on a hot summer day, there's something for just about everyone.

It's easy to take all of this for granted. But for much of the time since the area was settled in the late 1700s, the options described above were unimaginable to the majority of the citizens. They were too busy laboring in the factories and mills of Burlington and Winooski, or on the farms of other towns in the county. Long hours, with Sunday the only full day off for most, coupled with a lack of transportation options meant that most people just stayed home and rested during what little free time they had. Large families and meager wages meant that many struggled just to provide the basics. So even had time been available for recreation, the money often was just not there.

The coming of the railroad to the area in the mid 1800s greatly improved people's mobility. Well-to-do tourists from southern New England and New York started to come to the mountains of Stowe, or to places along the lake. Lake hotels sprang up on both sides of Lake Champlain, often of the spectacular variety. These hotels were usually serviced by a train depot and in some cases by a steamboat landing. But this travel infrastructure was largely for the well-off. To the working classes, leisure time was still an unknown concept. Train trips for working people were usually for things like day trips to visit relatives in nearby towns, or trips to Burlington to buy things not available locally. Even a trip to "local" attractions such as the ruins of Fort Ticonderoga or Ausable Chasm entailed a steamboat trip, then a railroad or coach trip along with a hotel stay. This was beyond the reach of most.

The coming of the first local public transportation, the horse railroad (1885), and soon after that the electric trolley car lines (1893) increased local mobility even more. But that increased mobility was largely limited to the towns served by the lines: Burlington, Winooski and Essex Junction.

The coming of the automobile was incremental. At first it was just an undependable curiosity, a toy for the rich. Even as car ownership increased, the lack of decent roads limited its impact. But by the 30s, car ownership and improved roads had reached the point where they ushered in the first chapter of what would be true revolution in lifestyle, as the family road trip became something that was within the reach of more and more families with each passing year. To serve this new market, numerous facilities quickly sprang up all over the county to accommodate these newly mobile and increasingly affluent travelers. We'll start our examination of Chittenden County's recreational infrastructure with a feature that could once be found just about everywhere.

Tourist Camps

"Tourist Camp" is just one of the many names given to the early places that offered low-cost accommodations to travelers, especially families, on an automobile road trip. These were also known as motor courts, tourist cabins, tourist cottages, etc. I'll use these terms interchangeably. They all followed the same basic model: a series of detached small wooden cabins clustered around the main building. The main building nearly always had gas pumps, a store, and usually a small restaurant or diner. The cabins were usually very spartan, as they were just stopping over spots for travelers, who typically stayed one night. But you could put up your family in a couple of cabins at a fraction of what a stay at a hotel would cost you. You could gas up, have a meal, buy some snacks and souvenirs, and be on your way. Unlike a hotel, tourist camps were seasonal, only open during the warmer months.

During the 30s and 40s the State of Vermont published a booklet titled *Vermont Tourist Homes, Hotels and Cabins*. I acquired several of these, but their listings are very incomplete as inclusion was voluntary. So precise numbers are not available, but just in Chittenden County there were probably at least 50 of these motor courts. There were at least ten in Malletts Bay, and Milton. Most were located right on the main roads, Routes 2 and 7. Three of the more memorable ones were located on the busy stretch of Route 7 between Shelburne and Burlington. They were so plentiful that a traveler could rely on the fact that if he couldn't get into one tourist camp, there would be another one a few miles down the road. So in the early days when many lacked a phone, having a reservation was not critical in planning your trip.

Some motor courts only had five or six cabins, but the economics of the business meant that most had many more than that. Champlain Park, four miles south of Burlington on Route 7, had 32 cabins. The Dutch Mill, a bit south of Champlain Park, had 25 cabins arrayed in a semi-circle around its distinctive main building that featured a Dutch-style windmill. Clarey's Bayside, at Mallett's Bay in Colchester, had over four dozen, along with a hotel-style tourist lodge.

While most tourist camps were places for a stopover by the side of a busy road, others were destinations. Most of the tourist camps at Mallett's Bay fit this description, as did Champlain Park. They were along the lake, and patrons of those camps generally came and stayed for extended visits to take advantage of the recreational activities offered by the lake.

I'll now feature several short histories of the more memorable tourist camps along with photos.

The Dutch Mill/Windmill Cabins

The Dutch Mill on Shelburne Road has been a familiar sight in the area for nearly 100 years. Like most tourist camps, it featured a main building with a small restaurant as well as gas pumps. Its windmill main building is a rare Vermont example of eye-catching roadside architecture that was common across the country in the first half of the 20th century. Overnight accommodations were in individual cabins arrayed around the main building, which featured an attention-getting windmill. The 25 original cabins were arranged in a semicircle tucked behind the windmill.

The Dutch Mill opened in 1928 on 25 acres, and at that time it had a panoramic view of the lake. The initial proprietor was a man named Clyde Irwin, who was a well-known area bootlegger during Prohibition, and in trouble with the law for many years during and after that social experiment. In 1930 he was in deep trouble with the law. Burlington Free Press reported in October of 1930 that eight weeks after her husband's escape from federal authorities on the way to prison, Mrs. Irwin sold the Dutch Mill complex to L.O. (Lynnford) Nye, who came from Highgate to run his new business venture. Mrs. Nye started selling antiques from the Dutch Mill.

In 1938 Mr. Nye died. The antique shop seemed to increase in prominence after that, as it was featured much more prominently in ads than the cabins were. In 1941 Charles Stetson, owner of the East O Lake Inn, bought the Dutch Mill. Apparently, the cabins had been allowed to deteriorate quite a bit and he conducted major renovations when he took over. When the tourist camp re-opened, Stetson gave it a new name, The Crescent Mill, apparently in reference to the half-moon arrangement of the cottages.

That new name did not last long. By 1946 the camp was known as the Windmill Cabins, although there were still frequent references to it as the Dutch Mill.

The record is a bit murky after that, but in 1968 Mr. and Mrs. Charles Bissonette acquired the property. They added 14 more cabins, bringing the total to 48. They also brought back the original name, the Dutch Mill, and the original blue color scheme. In 1972 they added a campground and some of the cabins were moved onto common foundations to create a motel, as the time of the tourist cabin had passed into history. In 1995 the Bissonettes added a restaurant in the windmill, which had served as the office for many years. Today the family continues to operate the restaurant, motel and campground. As far as I can tell there are no remaining individual cabins on the property.

Photo from the Lilian Baker Carlisle Collection, UVM Silver Special Collections.

The distinctive Dutch mill of the Windmill Motor Court in the early 70s.

Champlain Park/Champlain Motor Court

Champlain Park opened in 1933 just north of the Dutch Mill on the other side of Route 7. It featured a sandy beach and beautiful views of the lake and mountains to the west, so it was a destination motor court. Champlain Park must have been nice, because in 1936 Mr. and Mrs. William Seward Webb of Shelburne Farms engaged Champlain Park to house 26 guests who were in town for the wedding of their daughter Frederica. The guests also ate breakfast the day of the wedding at the Champlain Park restaurant. Since the Webbs could have put up their guests anywhere, it was pretty high praise that they selected Champlain Park.

So the first class accommodations and restaurant, along with a beautiful location and beach, proved to be a powerful draw. In 1939 proprietor Leo Schildhaus reported that 10,000 visitors had stayed at Champlain Park the summer before. Schildhaus was a Burlington physician who was also involved in real estate. He would later purchase and demolish the Frank R. Wells mansion, on a great estate in the heart of Burlington. Dr. Schildhaus moved to Florida in his later years and was attending physician at the hospital in Hollywood, Florida for Count Basie during his final illness.

Champlain Park changed hands several times, and by the mid 50s it was owned by well-known Burlington developer George Hauck. Hauck reported that it was still prospering at that time, as evidenced by the four new cabins he added to the property. In 1960 the name was changed to the Champlain Motor Lodge, and the units were reconfigured into four motel-style buildings. This enabled the business to last well into the motel era and compete with the numerous other motels on Route 7, but it marked the end of Champlain Park.

Photo from the James Detore Archive, UVM Silver Special Collections.

Champlain Park Motor Court, in 1957 in a view heading north on Route 7 in Shelburne. The main building signage emphasizes the word "Cabins."

Clarey's Bayside

Clarey's was much more than a tourist camp. It was a 25 acre recreation complex. George Clarey started the business in 1925. Initially he had a few cabins for rent, but the main attraction was his Bayside Pavilion, a large performance space/dance hall that featured traveling orchestras and bands from around the region. When the Big Band era blossomed, Clarey's hosted virtually every nationally known band leader during the 30s and 40s. Glenn Miller, Benny Goodman, Ozzie Nelson, Louis Armstrong, Duke Ellington, Tommy Dorsey, and many more all made the trek to Mallett's Bay. If there was no performance/dance scheduled, the pavilion doubled as a roller skating rink called Bayside Rollerway.

In addition to the pavilion, Clarey had a beautiful sand bathing beach on his property. He added a restaurant to serve the many customers flocking to his various attractions. As Bayside's popularity grew, Clarey dramatically expanded his business in 1939, adding 35 cabins, the previously mentioned tourist lodge, a hot dog stand, gas station, and a grocery store. He now offered a variety of cabins, with 30 cottages of three to six rooms, and 20 smaller cabins. All cottages and cabins featured hot showers and screened-in porches. From the basic unit to kitchenette models, cabins on the beach or in the woods, George Clarey had something for everyone no matter your budget or the length of your stay.

Bayside's dining room sat 100 people, and served breakfast, lunch and dinner. After dinner it became a "dine and dance" from nine to midnight every night. In later years Clarey added an arcade.

Clarey's for the most part was before my time. But I do have a vivid memory of it from the end-of-year picnic that my class at Burlington's Christ the King School enjoyed there not long before Clarey's burned. My memory is centered solely on their arcade. This feature was added toward the end of their run, but once I saw it, I was fixated. Two things I remember: They had one of those claw machines where you put in a coin and try to grab from the trinkets in the glass case. I had never seen one before, and I proceeded to pump nearly every nickel I had into it. My mother had given me some money, but it was probably no more than 50¢, maybe even a quarter. It wouldn't have mattered how much I had, it would have gone into that claw machine… except what I saved to buy a bag of those black pellets that turned into ash snakes when lit. Like the claw, I had never seen these before, and had to get a bag. When

Photo from The Penobscot Marine Museum.

Interior of Clarey's Bayside Dance Pavilion, where the biggest bands in America played and the locals danced throughout the Big Band Era.

Clarey's comes up in conversation, the roller skating and the big bands are the two things that people associate most with it. So my memory seems a bit silly, but that's what stuck with me as a ten-year-old.

If you didn't have a car, getting to Clarey's was still not a problem. During the season Burlington Rapid Transit, the area's local bus company, added Clarey's to its bus line. So for a dime in 1940, you could get to Clarey's from Burlington.

The Big Band era came and went, but Clarey's continued on. Roller skating, school picnics, and swimming at Bayside's beach provided memories that linger to this day. It all came to a sudden end when the Bayside complex was destroyed in a fire in 1964. The last major performer at the pavilion had been 31 year old Ray Charles, who appeared there on July 4, 1963. The cabins and many other smaller structures remained, but the time of the motor courts had passed. A few years later the cabins were auctioned off, and the land was sold to the town of Colchester. The former Clarey's Bayside is now Bayside Park, a public park and beach run by the town of Colchester.

But in its day, no other tourist camp could come close to the wide variety of recreation options available at Clarey's Bayside.

Photo from the Penobscot Marine Museum.

The sprawling recreation complex of Clarey's Bayside is seen in the 1930s. The many large and varied signs call attention to the offerings at Clarey's for food, lodging and entertainment.

Tahteyopah Lodge

Some tourist cabin operations are memorable because of their size and unique attractions, like Clarey's. Others, like the Windmill, featured a memorable main building. The cabins at Tahteyopah Lodge are probably not as well known, because they were set well back from Route 7, out of the view of drivers. The operation was small, just a handful of cabins, and there was no store, restaurant, gas pumps, or striking signage, which were characteristics of just about every other tourist cabin operation in Chittenden County. It's likely that very few today would recognize the name Tahteyopah Lodge, but perhaps they might remember these as Charlotte Marsh's cabins. These cabins are included here largely because their owner, Charlotte Marsh, was a unique character in the history of Chittenden County. Originally from Connecticut, she graduated from Middlebury College in 1918. She returned to Middlebury in 1920 and opened the Tea Time Tavern, a combination restaurant and tourist home. In 1932 she moved to South Burlington and opened her cottages to the public. According to Charlotte, Tahteyopah is "a Vermont Indian word that means 'the hostess greets you at the door'."

This references the fact that Charlotte lived on-site. The "main building" of the tourist camp was her home. Located one mile south of the Burlington line, she opened her small cabin operation to the traveling public. Tahteyopah was unusual because it lacked visibility, being set far back from the main road, a safety feature that Charlotte touted when pitching her cottages to families with small children. Adding to the appeal for such families were the playground, cribs and an abundance of toys that were available. Finally, Charlotte offered childcare from a college graduate (her) so parents could go on tours without them.

Her cabins were used by traveling Black artists who could not get rooms elsewhere in the local area. Duke Ellington stayed with her and became a lifelong friend. She ran the cabins until 1970. Described as outspoken, even blunt, she was passionate about her adopted home of South Burlington and any issue affecting it. She was described as the city's fiercest defender and sharpest critic. She always got right to the point, whether she was telling someone to put pecans, not walnuts, in their brownies, or arguing some point of local politics. Ms. Marsh was honored as Citizen of the Year at the Bicentennial celebration in 1976 for her total and selfless devotion to her community and the state of Vermont. She passed away at the age of 91, 15 years after ending her tourist cabin business.

Photo from the James Detore Archive, UVM Silver Special Collections.

Aerial view of Charlotte Marsh's cabins in the mid 40s. Her home is in the foreground.

Crocker's Woodland Cabins

George Crocker was originally from Massachusetts. He worked as a salesman for Texaco, and that brought him to Chittenden County. He took a liking to the area, especially Lake Champlain, as he was an avid boater and fisherman. He opened a Texaco station that was built in the Southwestern style with a Spanish tile roof, adobe-style walls, and other Southwestern accents. The station stood on the corner of Pearl Street and Elmwood Avenue, and was probably the most classic gas station ever built in Burlington.

He and his wife settled in Colchester, and in the summer they ran Crocker's Woodland Cottages and Cabins. These tourist cabins were in Malletts Bay, along what is now East Lakeshore Drive, about 200 yards from where Clarey's Bayside stood at the intersection with Blakely Road. Like other tourist camps along this stretch of road, most of Crocker's cabins were not on the water, but were located in the woods on the other side of the road from the beach. A few cabins were on the beach side, but their guests could enjoy the lake just a few steps from their cabin, no matter where it was located. Like nearly all tourist camps, Crocker's main building featured a small store and a snack bar, along with gas pumps. In a 1952 photo their sign in front advertised hot dogs, sandwiches, ice cream, and cold drinks.

Around 1954 Crocker opened another Texaco station, this one a modern one in the new Ethan Allen Shopping Center on North Avenue. The gas stations were his main source of income, but the Malletts Bay cabins were a side business of the Crockers for decades.

Photo from the James Detore Archive, UVM Silver Special Collections.

Several of Crocker's Woodland Cabins in 1952. The main building is on the left. Lake Champlain is on the other side of the road, a few steps away.

Motels

Area tourist camps prospered throughout the 30s, but the Second World War brought drastic changes to the area. Thousands of men left for the service and were destined to be gone for years. Strict rationing of gasoline and tires meant that recreational driving virtually ceased for the duration. It was so bad that the Burlington Country Club resorted to employing a horse and buggy to pick up golfers and take them to the course.

But the end of the war did not bring a revival for the tourist camps. The servicemen returned home, and those that didn't go to college under the GI Bill went to work in an American economy that stood astride the world. The defeated nations Germany and Japan had suffered near total destruction of their industrial base. But unlike most other wars, the victors too were flat on their backs. Great Britain took over a decade to begin to recover from the privations of the war. The Soviet Union's industrial base was wrecked. Of all of the pre-war industrial powers, only the American economy was untouched. Indeed, it had prospered, and with the war's end, that industrial might was turned toward peacetime production.

The result was a level of industrial dominance unmatched in human history. To give just one example, in 1945 the United States produced nearly three quarters of all the steel in the world. The result was that the middle class in America quickly grew much bigger and much more affluent. American consumers enjoyed the bigger and better cars that Detroit produced and that they were now able to afford. The American road trip came roaring back as American families hit the road in numbers unimaginable just a few years before.

But these newly affluent travelers were no longer content with the rustic cabins provided by tourist camps, which in many cases were only a bit better than camping. To meet the demands of the new traveler, motels sprang up like mushrooms in Chittenden County. The growth was staggering. In 1949 the word motel was still such a curiosity that it was bracketed in quotes when a newspaper story mentioned the term. The first Chittenden County establishment to use the term motel was the Paragon Apartments Motel that was built on the site of the Paragon Restaurant after it burned in 1949. They opened in the fall of 1950, but the term motel was a bit misleading. The sixteen units (1, 2, and 3 bedrooms) in the Paragon were more like apartments, as the long line of mailboxes in front of the building attested.

Regardless, dozens of actual motels would soon start to spring up in Chittenden County. The bed count of area motels went from zero in 1950 to 1800 by 1961, as over 40 new motels opened their doors. The bed count nearly doubled between 1959 to 1961. This phenomenal growth reflected national trends.

With so many new motels, a bit of an arms race ensued as proprietors added amenities to lure in customers overwhelmed by choices. By 1961 features such as telephones, television, free ice and in-room coffee became standard. Motel Pierre in Colchester really upped the ante in 1958 when they became the first motel to install a swimming pool. Many others quickly followed. Even by 1961 only half of the local motels were air conditioned. That would soon become standard as well.

Unlike the tourist camps, very few motels offered meals. By the 60s numerous dining options had opened along the same routes where the motels were located, so most felt no need to serve food. Only two motels in 1961 had restaurants, and a few others offered continental breakfast. So most motel operators felt that serving food was an unnecessary expense.

Most of these new area motels were clustered along the same roads as their predecessors, the tourist camps: Williston Road and Shelburne Road. In the twenty years after the war, of the dozens of motels that had sprung up in the area, nearly all were on Williston or Shelburne Road. Just about every one of these motels were locally owned. It would take the coming of the interstate to entice large chains like Holiday Inn and Sheraton to come to Chittenden County.

Some of the names of the motels referenced the area's historic past: The Ethan Allen, The Colonial Motor Court, The Yankee Doodle. Others evoked the beauty of the area: The Harbor Sunset, The Lakeview, The

Grand View. Others just emphasized a good night's sleep: The Sandman, The Night O Rest, and The Ho Hum.

While some of the motels from the 50s and 60s have been demolished, many are still standing. But while some are still standing, they haven't functioned as motels for some time. With the COVID-19 crisis, several were pressed into use as emergency housing for the homeless. This situation is still in play as this is being written.

Most of the early local motels fit the same basic pattern, a long one-story building featuring 10 to 20 units with an office at one end. Next I'll highlight a couple of the earliest of that type along with a few other motels that had more unique designs and histories.

Ho Hum Motel

The Ho Hum was one of the area's first motels, opening in 1951 on Williston Road. The location was ideal, on increasingly busy Williston Road, and very close to the airport. The design was U-shaped with modernistic rounded corners. The exterior was comprised of the bygone material called Homasote, and it was painted a light grey. There were 12 rooms: 10 singles with bathrooms and two housekeeping units with a living room, bedroom, kitchenette and bath. Owner Everett Nichols had relocated from Barre to design and construct the motel, which also included owner's living quarters. As this is being written, the Ho Hum Motel is still there but not currently operating as a motel.

Photo from the James Detore Archive, UVM Silver Special Collections.

The Ho Hum Motel on Williston Road shortly after it opened in 1951.

Del Ray Motel

The Del Ray opened in the spring of 1954 and was one of the first motels on Shelburne Road. Located at 1120 Shelburne Road, on the corner of McIntosh Avenue, the L-Shaped motel had 12 units. This layout was featured in most area motels, an office at one end with a long building (straight or L-shaped) of 10-20 units in it. Owner Leo Smith would open a second Shelburne Road Motel, the Town and Country a year later. He did not own the Del Ray for very long, selling it to the Barkers, a couple from Quebec, less than a year after it opened. The Barkers constructed a single family home next to the motel which would serve as their residence. Henry Barker would run the Del Ray Motel for 37 years. The motel was demolished in 2003, as was the Barkers' home, and a bank branch now stands on the site.

Photo from the James Detore Archive, UVM Silver Special Collections.

The Del Ray Motel right after completion in 1954. It was run by the Barkers, who would build their home next to their motel, just to the right of the driveway.

Redwood Motel

Located at 1016 Shelburne Road, when it opened in 1957 the Redwood was the largest motel in the area. It had 20 rooms and 32 beds, but it would get much bigger.

Designed, built, and operated by Howard and Laura Cranwell, the Redwood quickly became known as the best motel in the area. Howard Cranwell was a builder, and he would soon develop the Laurel Hill and Tanglewood Drive housing developments on the former Elmer Gove gladiola fields behind the Redwood.

Enter Elmer Premo. He had worked for 26 years in the bakery business, and was being transferred from Massachusetts to the Midwest. Not wanting to leave New England, he saw a listing for a motel and coffee shop in the

Burlington Free Press while visiting Middlebury. He bought the Redwood, retained the Redwood name, and two years later put on a 21-room addition, including a third floor "penthouse." The Redwood eventually expanded to 67 rooms, making it the one of the largest lodging sites in the area until the arrival of the national chains. The dining room became a destination even for those not staying at the Redwood. In the 80s the name changed to the Redwood Inn.

In 1994 it was purchased by Gabriel Handy, who made it part of the Super 8 motel chain. After that it was a Travelodge for a number of years.

Photo from the James Detore Archive/UVM Silver Special Collections.

The Redwood Motel complex is seen in this 1965 aerial view. To the right is the Val Preda Olds Cadillac dealership, and to the left are the buildings formerly used by Elmer Gove's Champlain View Gardens.

The Cupola Motel

The Cupola property had a rich history, including a long association with the Mary Fletcher Hospital. When the hospital opened in 1879, much of the food served to patients was grown in garden plots on the hospital property. But as the number of beds at the hospital grew, the acreage to grow food on hospital hill became insufficient. So in 1897 the hospital directors purchased the large Carlos Baxter farm, which ran along Williston Road from East Avenue to where the interstate is now. Baxter was a prominent attorney in early Burlington. The Baxter Farm became the Mary Fletcher Hospital Farm.

So for over 30 years the hospital steward would make daily trips to the hospital farm to bring back produce, chickens, milk, eggs, etc. to be used to feed their patients. The hospital finally stopped growing their own food and sold their farm to Fred Fiske in 1928. He farmed the land until 1952 when Roland Deslauriers of Brockton, MA bought the farm. He moved his family to Vermont, but soon found that he could not make a living farming. He returned to Brockton temporarily to earn the money needed to retain the farm, all the while planning to convert the century-old farm buildings into motel units. He returned in 1956 and opened his first nine motel units as work progressed on the many other buildings on the farm. Two hay barns, a carriage house, hen houses, a dairy barn, and the farm's homestead were all modernized, eventually becoming modern motel units save for the home, which became a restaurant and lounge. Family members did much of the renovation in addition to running the motel.

The old farm buildings featured eight distinctive cupolas which were retained and restored. According to legend, Carlos Baxter had them put up to beautify the farm at the insistence of his wife. Whatever their origin, the cupolas gave the new motel its name along with a very unique look. Initially only open seasonally, the Cupola evolved into a year-round 102-unit motel with a popular restaurant. In 1966 Roland Deslauriers sold the Cupola to the national Sheraton chain.

Donald Weidenmayer photo from the Vermont State Archives.

The Cupola Motel on Williston Road with its signature cupolas prominently featured. The former farm homestead is the restaurant seen in the photo.

Victorian Motor Inn

Like the Cupola, the Victorian Motor Inn was an historic property that was renovated by adding guest rooms. The original mansion was built in the 1860s by Lemuel S. Drew. Drew was an important figure in early Burlington, both as a hotel proprietor and for developing the streets on a parcel of land he owned around the current Drew Street, which bears his name. The mansion was in the French Second Empire style with the signature mansard roof. It sat in the middle of Drew's 250 acre stock farm on the Shelburne Road in South Burlington. Drew named it Lakeview Farm for its commanding views of the lake and mountains.

Eventually the house passed into the Bartlett family, for whom Bartlett's Bay is named. It served as the family home for decades. In the late 20s Mrs. George Bartlett started renting rooms in the mansion as a tourist home that she named "Elm Eden."

By the 60s the century-old mansion had been acquired by Bill Gabbeitt, a longtime restaurant owner in the Burlington area. He renovated the building, adding 15 guest rooms, each with a private bath, in addition to a large dining room and lounge. The Victorian Motor Inn opened for business in 1963, joining the many new motels already in business on Shelburne Road.

Gabbeitt sold the motor inn in 1975. After that several restaurants inhabited the main building. In 1984 a local developer bought the building

Photo from the Lilian Baker Carlisle Collection/UVM Silver Special Collections.

The Victorian Motor Inn on Shelburne Road when the Black Angus Steak House was the featured restaurant in the building.

and constructed a Howard Johnson's hotel next door. That building is currently a Holiday Inn Express. The old Victorian Motor Inn building continues to house a restaurant.

Queen City Motel

The main building of the Queen City Motel at 434 Shelburne Street in Burlington has an interesting history. This large brick Victorian mansion was built in 1881 at a cost of $7,000 for the Reverend Theodore Hopkins. He was the son of John Henry Hopkins, the first Episcopal bishop of Burlington. The Rev. Hopkins did not live long at his new home, as he died in 1889. The home had several owners, and then in 1952 a man named O.J. Rush constructed an L-shaped building on the property featuring 12 units and an office. This was located just north of the mansion, very close to Shelburne Road. The new motel was named the Queen City Motel.

In the late 80s the mansion was restored, converted to an inn, and incorporated into the motel as the Queen City Inn and Motel. The rooms in the restored mansion cost only $20 per night more than the rooms in the adjacent motel. In 1993 the bank foreclosed on the entire property. The 18-room mansion and the motel were sold to an environmental consulting firm. The mansion was converted to office space and the motel into apartments.

Author's collection

The Queen City Motel units and the associated Hopkins mansion are seen in this post card view.

Shopping

From the time that the area was settled in the late 1700s up until World War II, most retail commerce was between the waterfront and South Winooski Avenue. This included retail stores of various types: clothing stores, movie theaters, restaurants, soda fountains, drugstores, eventually car dealers, and just about anything else you could think of. If you lived in a rural area, which most of Chittenden County was up until the war, your town likely had a general store, a feed store, maybe a small millinery shop, and if you were lucky, a pharmacy in the village center. But if you wanted to buy something like toys, books, or other specialty items, it likely required a trip into Burlington. There was nothing in any of the surrounding towns that remotely resembled the large department stores that flourished on Burlington's Church Street from roughly 1880 to 1980.

For many years, shopping was almost exclusively something you did to acquire necessities. Only the well-to-do shopped for luxury goods and other non-essentials. But with the rise in affluence by the middle class after World War II, shopping became a pastime. Window shopping, browsing, and buying an item you wanted, not needed, became something that many did for enjoyment. Many long-standing stores adapted to this huge new market, and many others came into being to take advantage of the economic opportunities this change offered.

Next we'll look at some of the iconic department stores and specialty stores that were the "go-to" establishments from the 30s through the 70s and beyond.

Abernethy's

Abernethy's was regarded by many as the crown jewel of Burlington stores. Everything about it was first class. The magnificent Richardson Building at the top of Church Street was a fitting location for this splendid department store, which always claimed to date back to 1848. That was a bit of a stretch since it used precursor stores H.W. Allen, Lyman and Allen, and finally E.& E. Lyman to get back that far.

In point of fact, Frank Abernethy, the store's namesake, didn't come into the picture until 1880, when he moved to Burlington and started to work at Lyman and Allen. Lyman retired and H. W. Allen moved into the building at the top of Church Street known as the Richardson not long after it opened in 1897. He brought Abernethy, who was by then a partner, with him. Allen retired in 1910 and Abernethy took over the store. It was only then that it became Abernethy's, as Frank renamed it F. D. Abernethy. Due to several others buying in, it eventually became

Elliot Douglas.

Abernethy's Department Store in their ground floor space in The Richardson, the magnificent turreted building at the top of Church Street. Abernethy's painted signage on their south wall was a familiar sight on Church Street during the store's entire run downtown.

officially known as Abernethy, Clarkson & Wright. But to everyone it always was just Abernethy's. My mother, who worked there, always just called it "Ab's."

The store catered to what was known as the carriage trade. Abernethy's main customer base consisted of the wives of Burlington's well-to-do class. He made annual buying trips to Paris to make sure that his customers had the latest fashions. Frank Abernethy died in 1932, and the Wright family ran the store from that time forward. Abernethy's became more inclusive as it catered to the rising middle class. It had many departments featuring the finer things in life, a large China department, a bridal and formal department, and so forth. It also branched out with a men's department, a separate shoe department, etc.

But as time passed, even iconic Church Street stores like Abernethy's struggled to maintain their customers in the face of the many new shopping centers that opened in the 50s and early 60s with their acres of free parking. The store finally closed in the fall of 1982. Abernethy's was gone after 133 years in business, or 72, depending on which origin story you believe. In a sad footnote to the demise of the store, downtown merchants chipped in to decorate Abernethy's empty windows for Christmas in 1982 so that the top of the block would not look barren during the holidays.

Magrams

The story of Magrams department store starts with Max Glass, a Jewish refugee from Tsarist Russia who came to Burlington around 1914. He started as a peddler in the city but eventually opened a clothing store on Church Street called Union Clothing. In 1920 he renamed his store The Fashion Shop. This was a small Church Street storefront just south of F.W. Woolworth. In 1927 Barney Magram joined the Fashion Shop, relocating from Plattsburgh where he had been working at Merkel's Department Store. He was 21 years old.

Max Glass died in 1933 and his widow Rose continued The Fashion Shop. Barney Magram became the manager, running all aspects of the business. In 1943 he purchased a half-interest in the business, and that same year the business moved to much larger quarters in the Howard Opera House on the corner of Church and Bank. The Fashion Shop occupied most of the first two floors.

In 1952 Magram bought out the remaining 50% of The Fashion Shop and added his name to the business, which became known as Magrams, The Fashion Shop. In 1955 he modernized the store in a complete makeover, but in the new signage, the name Magrams was still subordinate to The Fashion Shop. In 1961 Magram bought the Howard Opera House from his longtime landlord, The Children's Home of Burlington. That institution had been gifted the building in 1904 by the estate of John Purple Howard, who had constructed the opera house in 1879.

Barney Magram built a strong reputation for personal service, and for having the latest fashions. He was a licensed commercial pilot, and would fly to New York often to keep up with the latest fashion trends. Women whose mothers had shopped at Abernethy's gravitated toward Magrams, whose style was seen as more in tune with modern times. The store expanded as other tenants of the opera house building left, and eventually Magrams occupied all four floors of the huge building. The Burlington store ultimately grew to 75,000 square feet, which put it on a par with large shopping center stores like Gaynes.

In 1958, due to ill health, Barney Magram turned the store over to one of his daughters, whose husband ran the store for 20 years. In 1974 the façade was remodeled again, and The Fashion Shop designation was finally

Photo from UVM Silver Special Collections.

Magrams Department store in the 1970s. At this point they occupied the entire Howard Opera House building. The travertine marble façade was installed in 1973 and was the last of several renovations of the ground floor level.

removed. The store signs just said "Magrams", reflecting what people in town had been calling it for years. Several Magrams branch stores had opened in cities in New York and Vermont. Magrams main store and branches employed over 300 people at its peak. Although it prospered during this time, eventually the store began to struggle. Reorganization efforts and the sale of their building could not save the store, which closed its doors for the final time on January 26, 1991.

Magrams was beloved not only by its thousands of patrons over the years, but also by its employees. A 2003 reunion of former Magrams employees that was held in a restaurant then occupying the basement of their old store attracted 47 people, some from as far away as California. That tells you what kind of store Magrams was.

One interesting note is that Magrams never used an apostrophe in their ads, while Abernethy's always did.

The Mayfair

The Mayfair was founded as the Mayfair Hat Shop at 104 Church Street in the 20s by J. Leo Schwarzbart, an immigrant from Germany. When he died suddenly in 1947 the store was taken over by his daughter Janet and her husband Hertzel Pasackow. Hertzel was from Grand Isle and had graduated from Burlington High School. He had been working at the Mayfair since returning from the service after World War II.

The Mayfair moved into a storefront at 108 Church Street in 1953. It was much larger than their previous location, which was two doors up the street. Pasackow expanded the line of merchandise to include sportswear and accessories. By this point the business was called Mayfair Millinery and was growing nicely, with stores in Plattsburgh and Rutland as well as the Burlington location.

The previous tenant of 108 Church was Miles and Riley. That well known Burlington men's shop had been burned out.

In 1961 the Mayfair moved again, this time across the street to 85 Church, the longtime location of the Humphrey's Blue Store. The new space was eight times larger than the original store and twice as big as the space at 108 Church.

One final move in 1968 brought the Mayfair to 25 Church Street, which was formerly People's Department Store. Somewhere along the way they had dropped the word "millinery" from the store's name. This is the location that most will likely remember. The storefront was renovated into an elegant Parisian look, with merchandise on two floors. The Mayfair was known as "the store with the green door." This had started at their 85 Church Street location and continued on with another green door at the new location.

The Mayfair closed in June of 1995 after nearly 70 years in business, all on Church Street.

Photo from the Fred G. Hill Collection/UVM Silver Special Collections.

The Parisian-style storefront of The Mayfair, "The Store with the Green Door," in the 1970s.

F. W. Woolworth's

Even though the dime store F.W. Woolworth's was a national chain, it's safe to say that their stores in downtown Burlington were as beloved as any local store that ever existed in the area. The first Woolworth's opened on Church Street in 1899. People still speak nostalgically about its creaky wooden floors and its lunch counter. My most vivid memory of the store was the wall of comic books on the south wall, and next to them were long licorice whips (unwrapped) hanging from metal hooks. Woolworth's featured an abundance of low-cost merchandise designed to appeal to kids through their adulthood.

After expanding the original store on the corner of Church and Cherry, eventually the old buildings housing Woolworth's were demolished in 1964 and a new, modern store opened that same year. Gone were the creaky floors, but a new "luncheonette" became a favorite spot for a quick bite. The 1964 store was reportedly the largest Woolworth's in New England when it opened.

But eventually the Woolworth chain started to struggle due to changing retail dynamics. They closed their Burlington store for the final time in November of 1998, ending their near century-long run on Church Street.

Photo from the James Detore Archive/UVM Silver Special Collections.

The new F.W. Woolworth store on Church Street is pictured in November of 1964, shortly after its grand opening. Seen across Cherry Street is Sears, which would leave downtown for Shelburne Road within a few months.

Hayes and Carney

In August of 1924 Arthur Hayes of Burlington and James Carney of New Haven, Connecticut opened the Hayes and Carney men's clothing store at 197 Bank Street (that building is now gone). In 1931 they relocated to the new Chittenden Bank Building next to the old Ethan Allen firehouse.

Burlington was blessed with many great men's clothier's over the years, and Hayes and Carney was one of the earliest and longest lasting. They featured numerous popular brands and always kept up with the latest trends. For many years they were the area provider for Boy Scout uniforms and related items.

The store stayed on lower Church until 1960, at which point they moved up to 50 Church. They did business there for another 30 years, finally going out of business in April of 1990, which ended their 66 year run selling men's clothes in downtown Burlington.

Photo from UVM Silver Special Collections.

Hayes and Carney at 50 Church Street, their last storefront downtown. The glass awning was installed as part of the Church Street Marketplace, which created a pedestrian mall downtown.

Shepard and Hamelle

John Shepard and Clement Hamelle had worked many years for Thomas Wright at Wright's clothing store in the old YMCA building at Church and College. When that building burned in 1928, destroying Wright's store, Hamelle and Shepard followed him to his next stop, F.D. Abernethy's store at 1 Church Street. After four years there, Shepard, with 27 years in the clothing business on Church Street, and Hamelle with 14, decided it was time to set out on their own. So, in October of 1932 they opened Shepard and Hamelle at 32 Church Street in a storefront recently vacated by another men's clothier, Thomas Clothing.

Shepard, who was a lot older than Hamelle, retired in 1949. Eventually Hamelle retired as well, leaving the running of the store to his son, also named Clement, but known as "Jack."

In 1952 they bought the Children's Shop, which had been in business since 1927 a few doors up Church Street from number 32. Shepard and Hamelle then moved into this location, "the 24 of Church Street," which is no doubt the location most people will remember. This gave them a much larger street level presence.

In an era when people dressed up a lot more, Shepard and Hamelle, along with Hayes and Carney, Nate's, and the men's shops at Magrams and Abernethey's, provided a wide variety of quality options for several generations of Burlingtonians.

Shepard and Hamelle closed in 1991 after nearly 60 years in business downtown.

Author's collection.

Shepard and Hamelle, one of Burlington's favorite men's clothing stores, at "the 24 of Church Street."

Nate's

Nate and Ben Harris were two brothers from St. Albans, and after graduating from St. Albans High School and spending a few years as a Western Union operator, Nate, with brother Ben, opened their first store in 1933. It was located in St. Albans and was called Nate's Green and Gold Shop. In 1938 the duo opened a second Nate's store in Montpelier. In the

40s they added a store in St. Johnsbury, and finally, in 1956 they opened their Burlington store, which was located in the Masonic Temple building at the top of Church Street. It would become the anchor of their small chain of stores. Their commercials often ended by rattling off their four locations: "Nate's: Burlington, St. Albans, Montpelier and St. Johnsbury." Their slogan was "Nate's, Vermont's Largest Men's Clothier."

Nate was very active in Burlington civic affairs, and a tireless promoter of downtown Burlington. Shortly after Nate died in 1977, the Nate Harris award was instituted in his honor. Every year it was presented to a local community member/retailer for their advocacy of downtown. Nate and winners of the award named for him can be seen on a plaque mounted in front of City Hall.

Ben, who lived in St. Johnsbury, and was therefore less visible than Nate in the Burlington area, outlived his brother by many years. He passed away in 2014 at the age of 101. He said that he had always wanted to live in Burlington, but settled in St. Johnsbury to run the store there and grew attached to the area.

In 1995 after 38 years at 1 Church Street, Nate's relocated to College Street. After two years at that location, Nate's closed its doors in 1997, ending their 40-year run downtown.

Author's collection.

Nate's and Nate's Connection are pictured in their longtime location on the ground floor of the Masonic Temple building at the top of Church Street.

The Tick Tock Shop

The Tick Tock Shop in Burlington was started by Bill Hazelett, the same Bill Hazelett who would move Hazelett Strip Casting from Connecticut to Colchester in 1960.

In 1944 he relocated from his native Cleveland to Burlington to work at Bell Aircraft. Bell Aircraft's Burlington plant wound down swiftly after the war, but Hazelett resolved to stay in town. He was an avid skier and boater, and he said that Burlington was the only town in the east that made both sports easily available.

He was mechanically inclined and had enjoyed repairing watches as a hobby since high school. Back before digital and battery powered watches, mechanical watches needed repair fairly often. Locals needing watches repaired often endured long waits due to a shortage of repair shops, so Hazelett decided to turn his hobby into a business. He hired one employee to get started. That employee was a young lady named Dawn Nichols. A year later they would marry, a union that lasted 63 years.

He secured space above Kresge's on Church Street. He then publicized a statewide contest to select a name for his new business. Two women each won $10 for suggesting the winning name, The Tick Tock Shop, which opened for business in January of 1946.

He advertised heavily, taking out daily ads in both the Free Press and the Daily News for the first couple of months in business. He was very confident in his ability, and each ad emphasized the expertise of the shop. All of this paid off quickly with robust business for the Tick Tock Shop. Less than three months after opening, he moved the shop's retail store down to the ground floor, taking space at 112 Cherry Street, just west of Sears and next door to B.F. Goodrich. All repairs were still being done at the space above Kresge's. In this same short period, the number of his employees increased to seven.

On his one year anniversary in business, Hazelett posted a report card on the Tick Tock Shop's growth in that first year. Employees had grown from one to thirteen. 8,356 watches had been repaired, and 643 new watches sold. Weekly volume of business was $1700.

In October of 1947 the Tick Tock Shop moved again, this time to 185 Bank Street, a space formerly occupied by Lawrence and Leclair. The new space was larger and closer to the center of Church Street. Hazelett employed seven watch repairmen, all WW2 veterans and all trained by him. Mrs. Hazelett was also still working at the shop and was also a trained watch repairer.

Bill Hazelett spent much of his time in Connecticut, lending his expertise to his father, who had been working to perfect a continuous metal casting machine for decades. In 1956 the elder Hazelett died, and Bill and his brother transferred the family business to Colchester. After that there is no mention of him in connection with the Tick Tock Shop.

We do know that he had sold Tick Tock by 1970 as the owners were listed as the Garbo (Gerber) family in reporting from that year. At this writing, the Tick Tock Shop, now known as Tick Tock Jewelers, is still in business at 185 Bank Street, and is still in the Garbo family.

Photo from the James Detore Archive/UVM Silver Special Collections.

The Tick Tock Shop in 1947 at their first ground floor location on Cherry Street.

Fishman's/Centers

Fishman's was a rarity; it was a significant Vermont based chain, M.H. Fishman Co., Inc. At its peak Fishman's had around 50 stores, from Maine to Alabama. Meyer Fishman was a Russian immigrant who came to the U.S. at 15, alone and unable to speak English. He got work on a Vergennes farm.

Photo from the Detore Archive/UVM Silver Special Collections.

The Church Street entrance to M.H. Fishman's in 1948 after a dramatic expansion and renovation of their antiquated 1929 storefront. The new look, which featured heavily veined white marble and glass blocks for light, could not have been more different from the previous look. This somewhat monolithic look was probably the most futuristic storefront ever to appear in downtown Burlington.

Two years later he had saved enough to buy a wagon and started peddling in Bristol. He opened his first Fishman's store in Rutland in 1917.

He had the good sense to move on from the five and dime designation of his competitors. His stores were more forthrightly labelled 5¢ to $1.00. When F.W. Woolworth's "five and dime" stores finally started selling items priced at more than 10¢, they received a lot of negative backlash.

M.H. Fishman's first storefront on Church Street opened in 1929. Its business model was exactly the same as its national chain competitors, Woolworth and Kresge, who were located directly across Church Street.

To enable Fishman's to better compete with the neighboring dime store giants, the store was expanded in 1948 to become L-shaped, fronting on Bank Street as well as Church. This increased the footprint of the store eightfold. It also saw the installation of one of the largest soda fountains ever seen in Burlington. The 1948 expansion also brought a revolutionary new look to Fishman's two storefronts on Church and Bank. The very dated 1929 storefront was replaced with an ultra modern front clad in heavily veined white marble with glass blocks for light. The new, much wider Bank Street façade had an identical look. These were probably the two most modern storefronts ever downtown, and they could almost be described as monolithic, although the beautiful marble helped to soften the look.

Fishman's was very popular with locals, and like their rivals, they carried almost everything, and always at low prices. That popularity was demonstrated by the fact that when W. T. Grant departed downtown for Shelburne Road, leaving their store adjacent to Fishman's vacant, Fishman's expanded further into the very large former Grant's store in 1961. At the same time, Fishman's was rebranded as Centers, which was a new discount division that Fishman's had initiated.

The massive former Fishman's store was completely destroyed in a 1974 fire.

Everyday Book Shop

The Everyday Book Shop got its start in 1927, when Miss Alice Blanchard opened her shop at 184 Pearl Street. She was a graduate of Smith College, and the two women she hired to help her in the shop were also Smith graduates. The shop was in the Clement building, which still stands near the corner of Winooski Avenue.

Miss Blanchard's store was the first one dedicated solely to books in Burlington, no stationery or other sidelines. She catered especially to children, with a wide array of children's titles and toys available for play in two children's corners, along with low chairs and tables to encourage kids to sit down and read something from the shelves. Book discussion groups at the shop became a regular occurrence during the winter. Alice herself became a regular speaker at the meetings of various groups, promoting reading and discussing new book releases.

In 1931 the shop moved to larger quarters at 213 College Street. Business was good. Five years later the shop was sold to Sanford Cobb, an editor with Publisher's Weekly in New York. His wife had worked with Alice in a book store in Northampton, Massachusetts many years before. After Alice sold the Everyday, she retired and went to live with her father Fred in Montpelier.

Cobb sold the bookstore in 1943. The new owners were a group of six shareholders, all from Burlington, with very familiar Burlington names such as Edmunds, Goss, Edlund, Appleyard, and Burgess. This group managed the shop for 12 years, but in 1955 it was sold again. This time the buyers were Mr. and Mrs. Edward Sanderson. He was with Brentano's in New York City. Sanderson, known as Ted, continued the tradition started by Miss Blanchard of giving regular talks in the community promoting books. All of the managers through these various changes of ownership also continued her practice of making the Everyday Book Shop a welcoming place for children.

Now onto the scene comes Elizabeth Orr, who for many is the name synonymous with the Everyday Book Shop. She was from England, and had dreamed of opening her own bookshop since she was a child. She emigrated to Canada, and with her husband James, worked in bookstores in Ottawa and Montreal. They decided that they wanted to run a bookstore in Vermont, and after looking in Woodstock and Middlebury, they came upon the Everyday Book Shop in Burlington. It was not for sale, but as Elizabeth Orr put it, "They convinced the owner (Ted Sanderson) that he was ready to sell." This was in the late 60s. She would end up running the Everyday Book Shop for 40 years, as long as all of the previous owners combined.

In 1971 they moved to larger quarters at 106 Church Street. The storefront was painted a bright yellow, and a large children's section was on the lower level. Kids quickly caught on to its huge selection of books and toys. Whenever we went there with our kids, they headed right down the stairs unprompted.

The Orrs divorced around 1976. James opened Orr's Hallmark Shop in the Burlington Square Mall, and Elizabeth continued to run the bookstore on her own. The store continued to do well for years thanks to a large and loyal local following built up over decades.

But over time, as large national chain bookstores such as Waldenbooks started to move into the area, local booksellers started to have a harder time. In 1994 the Little Professor, a longtime bookstore on Church Street, closed. The game-changing Barnes & Noble superstore opened on Dorset

Street in 1996. Burlington's answer was to recruit another national mega chain, Borders, to Church Street to at least try to keep some book business downtown. They opened in 1997.

Chassman and Bem's large bookstore in the Masonic Temple building was by far the largest local bookstore when Barnes & Noble and Borders opened. Its owner voiced confidence that he could withstand the onslaught from the megastore, but less than three years after the arrival of Barnes & Noble, Chassman and Bem closed. Soon only one locally owned bookstore was left. The Everyday Book Shop was still standing, although on incredibly wobbly legs.

Burlington Free Press Photo.

Elizabeth Orr's beloved Everyday Book Shop at 106 Church Street, before she had to move to a tiny space around the corner.

It stayed standing only because Elizabeth refused to quit. Her store was her life. In 2001, to save on rent, she moved from her beloved Church Street location to a tiny storefront around the corner on College Street. Unable to afford any help, she ran the store all by herself 12 hours a day, seven days a week. Each day she walked 2 ½ miles from her home on Spear Street. She never had a vacation during her final 15 years in business. Her only break was when a friend watched the store for two hours a week during her Tai Chi class. She had no family in Burlington. The store literally was her life.

This grueling schedule would be remarkable for anyone, but in her case even more so because she kept this up throughout her 70s. A small group of about 75 customers ordered all of their books, and most importantly, their daily out-of-town papers from her. This small but regular income was critical to enabling her to continue her shoestring operation. One of those customers summed up Elizabeth's Everyday Book Shop this way: "There's a gentility about it that's hard to match anywhere." Part of it was her British accent, but mostly what people loved about Elizabeth was her obvious love for books, for her customers, and for her quaint, tiny store. And of course, her indomitability.

But finally, after turning 80, it got to be too much. In 2008 she finally closed her shop. The Everyday Book Shop ended its run of 81 years in Burlington.

Hagar Hardware

Hagar Hardware was in business for 147 years, nearly all in downtown Burlington. By anyone's definition that makes it an iconic retailer.

The firm started in Shelburne in 1839 as Hagar and Comstock, Luther M. Hagar in partnership with George Comstock. In 1841 the firm moved to the corner of Church and College, where Leunig's has been for the last 40 years, and was called Hagar and Arthur. An early sign from that location just says "Hardware & Paints", no mention of Hagar. In 1857 the partnership with Arthur was dissolved, and the following year Luther Hagar's son George I. Hagar joined him in the business, creating the firm of L.M. & G.I. Hagar.

George Hagar served admirably in the Civil War. When President Lincoln called for 75,000 volunteers, Hagar was the first person in Burlington to enlist. He served as a lieutenant before being mustered out after his 90 day commitment was up. A year later he re-enlisted as a private and served until mustered out again shortly after Gettysburg with the rank of sergeant major. He would be a very active member of Burlington's GAR post the rest of his life.

After the war, George returned to the hardware business, and in 1868 the store moved one door west on College from the corner they had occupied for 27 years. In 1870 his father retired, so George became the sole proprietor, doing business as George I. Hagar.

The business prospered for the next three decades under George's management. But it all came to a sudden end one morning in late February of 1899. George was at the GAR post preparing to march in the funeral procession for a fellow Civil War veteran. He went over the post's roster and drew a line through the name of the deceased, remarking "another poor comrade mustered out." He then walked across the room, sat in a chair, and died of a heart attack.

Just a few days after Hagar's death, ads for his hardware business started to appear again in the newspaper. For its entire run in business Hagar's was a heavy user of newspaper advertising. On March 6, an ad for bicycles appeared, and instead of George I. Hagar, the business was listed as the Estate of George I. Hagar. For three years the status of the business appeared to be in limbo, at least based on their advertisements. Some ads used the old name, while others listed the "estate of."

Finally, in 1902 the status was resolved when the Hagars announced that the business name was being changed from George I. Hagar to Hagar Brothers. George's two sons, Henry H. Hagar, and Charles H. Hagar, who had been running the business for the estate since their father died, officially took over the reins. In 1909 the name was changed once more as the business incorporated as the Hagar Hardware and Paint Company. Paint had become a huge part of their growing business, particularly their wholesale division, which was selling a great volume of paint all over the state. Hagar secured exclusive distributorship rights for national brands such as Kyanize.

1922 was another significant year for the firm as they moved their retail store into the space of a former hardware store at 98 Church Street. They would occupy that space for the rest of their run. A year later they moved their wholesale division to a large brick building at 164 St. Paul Street (corner of King).

Photo from the James Detore Archive/UVM Silver Special Collections

Hagar Hardware's old storefront on Church Street in 1965, right before their huge overhead neon sign was removed.

In 1928 Henry Hagar died. His brother Charles had not been involved in the firm for a number of years. He had always been more interested in boats, and eventually became a steamboat captain on Lake Champlain, piloting vessels toward the end of the steamboat era, including Vermont III and Ticonderoga. Because of this, Henry had brought in Frank J. Whalen to help manage the company. Upon the death of Henry in 1928, Whalen became president, the first non-Hagar to run this business since it started 89 years earlier.

Whalen ran the company until his death in 1951. At that point a fourth generation Hagar took over as another George I. Hagar, the great grandson of Luther Hagar, became president. He retired in the late 70s and his son G. Henry Hagar became president, the fifth and last generation of Hagars to run the company.

In the company's later years they branched out into automotive supplies, selling auto parts at their St. Paul Street location and at two branches in Essex Junction and Newport. Eventually they would operate five Napa Auto Parts stores.

The company had many long time employees, best exemplified by Ralph Thomas, who was vice-president of Hagar Hardware when he died in 1978. He had started there in 1917 and was still working when he died at 86. John Potter of Burlington, who worked at Hagar's for 45 years said "Mostly anybody who started, stayed with Hagar's. It was a family affair."

In late 1986 Leonard and Elaine Hanson of Ludlow purchased the store and changed the name to Hanson's Hardware. That brought an end to the 147 year run of Hagar Hardware, by any definition an iconic Burlington business.

Mazel's and Gaynes

Morris Mazel had started as a peddler, selling goods from a horse-drawn wagon in the North Street area. In 1914 he moved his business into the old Gosselin Drug Store building at 194 North Street. In 1936 Morris Mazel brought his three sons, Frank, Lou and Sid into the business.

In 1940 the store was expanded from 2,500 square feet to 9,000, and Mazel modernized the storefront. He installed a modern Carrara glass facade over the front of the pre-1900 building, and the ivory colored glass gave the store a bright, modern appearance. The word "Mazel's" in modern green script completed the new look. A large new Art Deco-style neon sign was hung from the top two floors of the building.

Unfortunately all this did not last long, as a fire devastated Mazel's less than six years later. The fire burned out Mazel's, and the back of the building, which was 165 feet deep, collapsed.

Undaunted, the Mazels quickly rebuilt. A new, bigger Mazel's was constructed by Kieslich Construction. It expanded the store to 13,500 square feet and again featured a very modern, sleek storefront.

After running Mazel's with their father for a number of years, in 1958 Sid and Lou (Frank had died in 1947) announced that they would be opening a new 25,000 square foot discount department store in the Green Mountain Shopping Center on Williston Road near the soon-to-be-built interstate

Photo from the James Detore Archive/UVM Silver Special Collections.

Mazel's Department Store on North Street after their 1800s building was given a modern makeover. The new front of cream-colored Carrara glass with green letters gave the storefront a sleek design. A large overhead Art Deco neon sign completed the look.

cloverleaf. They said that they would have called the store Mazel's, but the North Street store was still in business, so they opted for "Gaynes", which they said was a short and attractive name.

In 1961 Gaynes more than doubled in size to 55,000 square feet, reflecting the robust growth in Chittenden County's retail sales. By 1963 the store had expanded again to a massive 80,000 square feet. Many of the departments were leased out to independent operators, including shoes, hardware and paint, the garden center, the automotive center, toys, fabric, and the pharmacy. The store also featured a beauty salon and a barber shop.

After Morris Mazel died in 1965, the brothers wound down the North Street department store by the end of 1969, and it became Mazel's Shoe

Store, which continued in business until 1982. Lou Mazel ran Gaynes after Sid died in 1971, but finally sold the business to a Massachusetts firm in 1985, bringing an end to over 70 years of memorable Mazel retailing in Burlington.

Lou Mazel died in 2012 at the age of 99.

Bailey's Music Rooms

Bailey's Music Rooms was a longtime Burlington institution. Bailey's actually started in St. Johnsbury. It was founded in 1869 there by Alden Lee Bailey. Born in Quebec and orphaned at ten, he was "bound out" to work on his uncle's farm for the rest of his minority. Once he was grown, he was determined to make a success in business, and was 24 when he started Bailey's Music Rooms. Two years later he opened a branch in Burlington. It was managed by Col. H.W. Hall and located at 151 Main St., just to the left of where the Flynn Theatre currently is. At that time

Photo from the James Detore Archive/UVM Silver Special Collections.

Bailey's Music Rooms at 88 Church Street in a classic nighttime shot from 1948. Bailey's was Burlington's store for all things music for generations of local residents. They moved here in 1943 and were at this address until they closed in 1983. It was the last of their five locations downtown.

Burlington was a booming lumber, manufacturing, and transportation center. It was the state's largest city and growing rapidly. In those days before radio and recorded music most well-to-do homes had a piano or an organ. There were many well-to-do homes in late nineteenth century Burlington. Bailey's biggest business was pianos, organs, and sheet music, and business was excellent. The Burlington location moved to larger space in the old YMCA building at 171 College Street. The YMCA building burned in 1928, and Bailey's moved to 217 College Street and then to 159 Bank Street. In 1943, after 72 years in Burlington at four different locations, Bailey's finally moved to the location that everyone who remembers Bailey's associates them with: 88 Church Street.

All this time, A. L. Bailey's firm was expanding rapidly. There were Bailey's Music Rooms in St. Albans, Morrisville, Barre, Glens Falls and Gloversville, NY. Later Bailey added stores in Lancaster and Plymouth, NH. He employed twenty traveling salesmen in addition to store employees. Burlington was by far the biggest location, with a dozen traveling salesmen based there and another twelve working at the store. Bailey's was always a leader in featuring the latest in music offerings, being a licensed dealer for Atwater Kent radios, RCA Victrolas, Gibson guitars, and other top brands. When records became the way people bought music, Bailey's was the only store with listening booths where you could listen to a record before deciding whether to buy it. During the Depression they sold appliances such as washing machines to stay afloat during those tough times. In the 70s they sold color televisions.

A.L. Bailey never left St. Johnsbury. He died there in 1921 and is buried there. Eventually all the locations except for Burlington closed. Bailey's prospered through the advent of 78 rpm records, the Big Band era, and was the go-to store for records through the rock era boom times of the 60s and 70s. Finally, after a 122 year run in Burlington, Bailey's Church Street shop closed its doors in November of 1983.

F.J. Preston & Son Jewelers

Preston's business history goes back to 1840 when Adams Preston started a jewelry store in Bradford, Vermont. His nephew, named Lafayette Preston, worked for him and was the founding father of the family line that would run Preston's in Burlington. Lafayette opened his own store in Brandon in 1844, later moving to Castleton, where he ran a store for 40 years, with branches in Fair Haven and New York state. The firm dated their founding from the opening of Lafayette's first store.

Lafayette's youngest son was named Frank James Preston, and he moved to Burlington in 1903 to take a job as a musician at the newly-opened Strong Theatre. Frank was an accomplished pianist and became a member of the Strong's orchestra, playing for musical productions and later silent movies. He was also a violinist in the Burlington Symphony orchestra. He also played the cornet and drums and was an expert telegraph operator, so he had a lot of career options. For several years before coming to Burlington he made a living as head of a musical troupe that toured the eastern U.S.

He was 36 years old in 1903 and had grown up in the family business. So to supplement his income he went to work as an engraver at Bero Jewelers, which by that point was owned by his cousin George Preston.

In 1913 Frank left Bero's and opened his own small store at 3 Church Street, in the Masonic building in a space he shared with the C.H. Spear Company. Frank's space included "the north window" for displaying his wares. Assisted in running the store by his 18-year-old son, William S. Preston, Frank was able to continue as a musician at the Strong. The new

Photo from the James Detore Archive/UVM Special Collections.

The new store of F.J. Preston & Son Jewelers is pictured in 1964 after it was rebuilt following a fire that destroyed the business. This was Preston's final storefront.

store was known as F. J. Preston & Son.

In 1916 he moved into a larger space at 17 Church, a few doors down from his first location. The business prospered, adding an optical department, sterling silver services, and a repair department.

Frank Preston died in 1944, and his son and grandson, William S. Preston Sr. and Jr. continued running the business effectively. Both became president of the American Gem Society and served in other national positions. Preston's came to be synonymous with quality, value, and service.

In 1955 the business was expanded, adding 15 Church Street to the store's footprint. In early 1963 a fire destroyed the interior of the store, but customers' jewelry and precious gems on site were all safely stored in vaults. The fire caused Preston's to hold the first sale ever in their 50-year history on Church Street. After renting for 47 years the Prestons purchased their premises when the owners declined to rebuild. After nearly a year of renovations a new F. J. Preston's store opened in November of 1963.

William S. Preston Jr. retired in 1992 after 50 years with the business. Unfortunately F. J. Preston & Son would not survive for very long after his departure. On September 21, 1994 the Howard Bank took possession of the store's inventory, which had been put up as collateral for a loan. A number of liens had already been filed by suppliers for non-payment. The following day a throng of nervous customers was lined up when the store opened, anxious to retrieve items they had left for repair or appraisal. Rumors had been swirling about the situation at Preston's for some time, and the Howard Bank's action confirmed the worst. Two days later it was announced that the store's inventory and fixtures would be liquidated. A going out of business sale was held and by October 11, 1994 Preston's 150-year run in the jewelry business came to a sad end.

McAuliffe's

The distinctive stone entrance to the former McAuliffe building on the corner of Church and College commemorates two longtime Burlington companies that shared a lot of history.

The firm listed on top is Samuel Huntington, which was a book bindery and stationery store that started in business in 1837. They occupied this spot for decades.

Patrick McAuliffe went to work in Samuel Huntington's store in 1886 at the age of 13. Less than a year later the entire block was destroyed by fire. Samuel Huntington, in partnership with the YMCA, rebuilt a bigger and better store of sandstone and brick in what would come to be known as the YMCA building.

Over the years the store on the corner passed through several other hands, but it was always a stationery/book store. In 1912, McAuliffe started the McAuliffe Paper Company at another location on College Street. After seven years there, and then on Church Street, McAuliffe returned to his roots and purchased the Corner Book Store, which then was the name of

Photo from the Fred G. Hill Collection/UVM Silver Special Collections.

McAuliffe's classic brownstone and brick building shortly after McAuliffe's went out of business. This structure replaced the much larger Huntington/YMCA building that was destroyed in a 1928 fire.

the firm occupying the corner of Church and College.

In 1928 the YMCA building was destroyed in a memorable fire. McAuliffe rebuilt his store there and re-used the stone from the earlier building for his entrance. The two columns flanking the entrance still show charring from the 1928 fire.

Huntington's name is still there, but now it was joined by the McAuliffe name. The date 1912 on the lintel is when McAuliffe's started, and 1928 was the year the former building burned. McAuliffe's obviously had a lot more years in them. In 1936 Patrick McAuliffe celebrated 50 years in the stationery business and he was still only 63. By then the company had grown significantly, and had another large building at 67 Main that was their wholesale operation. They really kept it in the family; all four company officers at that time were McAuliffes.

In 1972 Patrick McAuliffe's grandson Michael Kehoe purchased the building and continued to run it for a while as the Corner Book Store. By 1982 he had converted it into a menswear store.

McAuliffe's brownstone building is a Burlington landmark, and the building is still referred to by that name by most longtime residents.

Fremeau's Jewelers

When Fremeau's Jewelers closed in 2016 they ended a run of 176 years, all on Church Street, which made them one of the longest-running businesses ever in the history of Burlington.

The firm was founded by Louis Xavier Fremeau, who was born in Montreal

Photo by Rebecca Williams/National Archives.

The large, modern storefront that Fremeau Jewelers moved into after their old store was destroyed by fire. The new building opened in 1976 and housed Fremeau's until they closed in 2016.

in 1822 and as a youth spent several years in New York City training as a watchmaker under a European craftsman at a large jewelry firm in the city. Louis made his way to Burlington, setting up shop around 1840 on Church Street and first advertising his business in 1848. Fremeau's always dated their founding from 1840. The business would continue under Louis' son and grandson, Louis X. Fremeau II and III. Other family members would be involved as well as the business continued into the 20th century. After occupying several locations on Church Street, Fremeau's finally settled in at 74 Church Street in 1919. They would occupy this space, except for disruption by a fire, for the remaining 97 years that they would be in business.

The name evolved from Louis X. Fremeau, to Fremeau Brothers, and finally to simply Fremeau's.

In 1959 Louis X. Fremeau III sold the store to Warren Wood of Middlebury. He wisely retained the name of the 120-year-old business. Fremeau's continued to do business in the small and antiquated storefront at 74 Church Street.

But that would change in July of 1974 when Fremeau's was one of several businesses that were destroyed in the massive Centers fire. In short order, the old storefronts on that section of Church Street were replaced by a two story modern brick business block. Fremeau's moved into a large space in the block with a corner entrance on Bank and Church Streets. They remained there until 2016 when Kent Wood, Warren's son, decided to close Fremeau's, mainly because no one in the Wood family wanted to continue as the third generation running the business. So Fremeau's 176-year tenure on Church Street came to an end in the autumn of that year.

It's interesting to note that the longest tenured businesses on Church Street were both jewelry stores. Fremeau's, at 176 years, is the champ, but right behind was Brinsmaid's/Bero's at 174 years. Preston's was in business for over 150 years, but only 80 of those years were in Burlington. Lippa's, which started in 1936, has been on Church Street for 87 years, and is still in business at this writing.

Wood's Sporting Goods

Lyman P. Wood came to Burlington in 1894 as a salesman for an Ohio tobacco company. In 1899 he opened his own cigar store on Church Street, at the corner of Bank. 1906 brought the first indication that Wood was venturing into sporting goods, as an ad from that year offers tennis equipment. Later that same year he advertised football equipment for sale.

But the store was still primarily a tobacconist, with most ads being for cigars, pipes, etc. It sold other items almost randomly; safety razors, newspapers, phonographs, typewriters, in addition to some sporting goods. But gradually sporting goods assumed more of a presence, and in 1910 for the first time the store was billed as Wood's Sporting Goods.

You can see the store's transition in photos taken of it over time. One from 1911 shows the main store sign as L. P. Wood Sporting Goods and you can see tennis rackets in the window. Another sign indicates that Wood's was an agent for Columbia bicycles. But this early, the majority of the signage was still for cigars and tobacco products.

Wood's store on Church Street evolved more and more into sporting goods and away from tobacco. But even years later, when Wood's Sporting Goods had become the most important seller of sports equipment in the area, he still featured non-sports items like cigarettes, newspapers, cameras and office equipment, particularly typewriters.

Photo from the James Detore Archive/UVM Silver Special Collections.

Wood's Sporting Goods occupied the northeast corner of Church and Bank Streets for their entire existence, from 1898 to 1971. The store is seen in the 40s.

L.P. Wood sold his sporting goods store a month before his death in 1941. It continued its successful run under the new owner, Sabin Abell, who emphasized sporting goods over the many other items that L.P. Wood had featured in the store, although cameras continued to be a focus. Abell grew Wood's into a dominant force in sporting goods in Chittenden County. They sold equipment from every sport imaginable and outfitted many local teams.

In 1955 Abell renovated the store, installing a modern sign with large red block letters replacing the antiquated signage from another era.

In 1966 the firm of Mills and Greer was formed, and they began making inroads in competing with Wood's, which had for so many years been the go-to sporting goods house in the area.

Abell sold the store in 1970. In an eerie echo of L.P. Wood, Abell died a couple of months after selling Wood's Sporting Goods. Abell's son, Sabin Jr., who had been managing the store, ceased his involvement once the business changed hands. The block containing Wood's and other businesses was sold to Warren Wood (no relation). He announced plans to renovate the entire block. But less than two years after Sabin Abell sold Wood's, it went out of business in mid-1972.

In July of 1973 the Howard Bank opened a new branch on the renovated corner where L.P. Wood's had stood for so long.

In July of 1974 the newly renovated block was destroyed as collateral damage in the Centers Fire. An account of the fire indicated that the building that had formerly housed Wood's Sporting Goods was the oldest building on Church Street, having been built in 1805.

Forest Hills Factory Outlet

When the American Woolen Company closed their mills in Winooski in 1954, it presented the city with two huge problems. One was the loss of hundreds of jobs by the local people who had worked at the mills, in some cases for decades. The other was what to do with the complex of former mill buildings, some of them gigantic, that would soon be vacant. Finding someone to occupy such large spaces was going to be a huge challenge, but it had to be done as quickly as possible. Empty factories tended to attract vandals, and could quickly become eyesores.

Into the breach stepped a regional chain known as Forest Hills Factory

Outlets. The company was headquartered in the Boston area and had been in business since 1910. The chain's stores were mostly in New England, although they had at least one in New York. Their latest outlet in Winooski opened in 1957 in the former mill building located on West Canal Street, now the Woolen Mill Apartments.

When Forest Hills opened, there was only one shopping center open in the area, although others would soon follow. Forest Hills had many of the advantages that the shopping centers offered, and that downtown Burlington's stores lacked. It had acres of free parking, space for over 300 cars. It also offered just about everything under the sun, all under one roof. This was before Grand Way or Gaynes, so when it opened, Forest Hills was the largest department store in the state. And of course, as a discounter, the prices at Forest Hills were extremely attractive to locals.

A large (80 feet long) sign was attached to the top of the side of the woolen mill building facing the river. It was easy to spot by anyone coming to Winooski from the Burlington side. Full page ads trumpeted the opening of Forest Hills, which was in many ways, unique to the area in 1957.

The store's former mill building had been built on land that originally sloped steeply down from West Canal Street to the Winooski River. So one of the features that many remember was its long concrete ramp leading down to the lower level of the store.

Forest Hills Factory Outlet on West Canal Street in Winooski not long before they closed in 1978. Note the associated laundromat in the front. Photo from the Vermont State Archives.

Forest Hills had dozens of departments, several of which were run by licensed independent operators, such as cameras, the hobby department, the auto center, sporting goods and the music department. There was a snack bar, a laundromat, and a grocery store. The grocery store was memorable enough to merit its own entry in this book, and that follows this one.

Just the furniture, appliance and floor-covering departments occupied 40,000 square feet of space. Shortly after opening, Forest Hills added 30,000 additional square feet. So Forest Hills was enormous, and the cavernous spaces that it occupied felt even larger due to the very high ceilings of the old mill buildings.

In 1962 Grossman's, New England's largest building material chain, which was based in Massachusetts, opened an outlet at Forest Hills. They were located in a section of the mill that ran along the river, across the parking lot from Forest Hills. Their front entrance was down a steep driveway that led to the parking lot.

In 1975 Grossman's left Winooski for Bartlett's Bay Road in South Burlington. By this point the area was overflowing with shopping centers, and was home to several dozen department stores of all types, local, regional and national chains, from high-end stores to discounters like Forest Hills. The advantages that Forest Hills had enjoyed in the early years were long gone. In nearly all cases, their competitors featured more modern stores that were easier to get to, nicer, and easier to park at. Large local discounters Gaynes, Grand Way, and Centers had been eating into their share of that market for years. So it didn't come as a big shock to many when it was announced in 1978 that Forest Hills Factory Outlet was going out of business.

The Country Store

While it's a bit of a stretch to include a grocery store in a book about recreational activity, I couldn't do this book and leave out the grocery store at Forest Hills Factory Outlet. Their grocery department set the Winooski Forest Hills apart from all of the chain's other outlets. In 1959 Merle Wood relocated his Country Store from Essex to Forest Hills. He would soon open other Country Stores in Fair Haven and Berlin. Wood operated his Country Store in Winooski as an independent operator. The store occupied 15,000 square feet, and in a foreshadowing of Costco, offered great deals for volume purchases.

What made the Country Store so memorable was Wood himself. He was famous for his one minute commercials broadcast on local TV station WCAX. Wood started doing TV in 1955 with a live one minute spot for his Essex store, shown once a week at 6:30 on WCAX, between the local news and Walter Cronkite. One year after his first TV commercial, his business tripled. From that point forward he never advertised in print again, putting all of his ad dollars into television. His TV ads expanded from once a week to six nights per week. He would come to the station to do the commercial, put on a white grocer's apron and paper Holsum Bakery cap, and proceed to work his way through a table filled with grocery bargains in a style that some have likened to that of a carnival barker. Seven loaves of bread for $1, the same price for three pounds of hamburger, 50 pounds of potatoes for 99¢. He would speed-talk his way down the entire table, emphasizing the value of every item on that table. He had the whole thing down to a science. He never ran short of time, always squeezing every item on the table into that minute that he had purchased from WCAX.

Photo by Hanson Carroll from Vermont Life Magazine

Merle Wood geared up for one of his TV spots on WCAX television. His prices were unbeatable, and his commercials were unforgettable.

By 1961 his sales volume had increased fivefold from 1957. Part of that increase was due to his new location, but a lot of it was due to his commercials, which by now were a familiar part of just about everyone's nightly TV viewing. Burlington wholesale grocer S.R. Saiger said that Wood's three stores accounted for 25% of his entire wholesale business.

Wood's pitch, though speedy, was always easy to understand. People loved his unbeatable prices, and even though you had to purchase large quantities to get those deals, buying seven loaves of bread or 50 pounds of potatoes was not a problem for many at a time when very large families were common. Wood was one of the more colorful characters ever to appear on the Chittenden County scene. His commercials seem to be the thing that many people remember most about Forest Hills. I can still hear his voice in my head clearly after all these years.

Merle Wood died in 1967 at 54 years of age. With him gone, there was no one who could replace him in the TV commercials, so the Country Store resumed print ads, running huge full-page spreads for the specials previously touted by Wood. But it just wasn't the same. The Country Store at Winooski hung on for a few more years, but was out of business early in 1973. A new grocery outlet at Forest Hills called the Quality Warehouse Market took their place, but they folded when Forest Hills closed in 1978.

The Shopping Centers

The dawn of the consumer age and the car culture went hand in hand, sweeping the nation as post war families grew and prospered. One dramatic result of this was the rise of the suburban shopping center. Urban downtowns big and small had been the retail centers for many years as large locally owned department stores, often in ornate landmark buildings, had been the main draw for generations of shoppers. Many smaller shops augmented these iconic stores, providing just about anything that you could need or want.

But after the war, developers started acquiring cheaper land well outside downtown cores, and erecting shopping centers. These featured a large variety of store types, usually with one or two large national chains as anchor

Photo from UVM Silver Special Collections.

The Ethan Allen Shopping Center on North Avenue shortly after opening. Original stores visible in the photo include a Grand Union supermarket, McKane's appliance store, a Ben Franklin 5 and 10 cent store, and a Burlington Savings Bank branch.

stores. They were large, usually one-story buildings, often containing dozens of different stores. These low buildings were easily customizable to enable the developer to meet the changing needs of retail tenants. And of course, a main draw was the acres of free parking.

Contrast this with the traditional downtown, where parking was often difficult, and nearly never free. The gorgeous landmark stores of generations past were just about impossible to customize due to their ornate construction and historic nature.

As with most national trends, Vermont was a bit behind the curve when it came to shopping centers. The first one built in Chittenden County was the Ethan Allen Shopping Center on North Avenue in Burlington, which opened in 1954. While not in the suburbs, it was far enough from downtown that open land was still plentiful. Built by the Hauke brothers, Bill and Roland, it was managed by Tony Pomerleau, whose business success would come to be synonymous with Vermont shopping centers over the following years.

Ethan Allen featured a Grand Union supermarket and a Ben Franklin department store as its anchors. Other stores included a bank, cleaner, drug store, bakery, coffee shop, and appliance store. Many more stores would soon follow. The parking lot featured 250 spaces. A large bowling alley, the Ethan Allen Lanes, would soon be built behind the building housing the stores. Within a few years it would be expanded from 18 to 24 lanes, making it the largest bowling alley ever in Chittenden County.

The location was also convenient to what is known as the "New North End" of Burlington, which was rapidly being developed at this time.

Photo by Donald Weidenmayer/Vermont State Archives.

Grand-Way in the Seaway Shopping Center, a mega store by local standards, is seen with its large block letter signage in 1963.

Meanwhile, at the other end of Burlington, Thomas Farrell had acquired the old Wabanaukee golf course property, located at the far southern Burlington city limit. By 1955 he had built a large Grand Union supermarket, along with an office building on the section of the old golf course nearest to Shelburne Road. He also renovated the old Wabanaukee clubhouse into what he named the Olde Board Restaurant. Farrell quickly announced plans to add a mega store next to the newly opened Grand Union.

Construction on this store, Grand Way, started in 1959. At 60,000 square feet, when it opened it was the largest store ever in Vermont, a title it would not hold for very long. Grand Way was a discount department store that was a division of the Grand Union company, with whom Farrell already had a working relationship. Along with Grand Union and Grand Way, Farrell also built several detached buildings, one of which lured the Agel-Corman furniture store from downtown into Farrell's new shopping complex, which he dubbed The Seaway Shopping Center. Presumably this was named for the St. Lawrence Seaway, which was in the news at the time. The parking lot accommodated an almost unimaginable 700 cars, with lots both in front of and behind the stores. The Seaway Shopping Center would be the only one of Chittenden County's five early shopping centers which Tony Pomerleau did not either own or manage.

With the decision by IBM to locate a plant in Essex Junction, the Hauke brothers and Tony Pomerleau targeted that area as the location for their next shopping center. They purchased six acres of land just east of the Champlain Valley Fairgrounds. Construction began in the fall of 1957 and the first segment of eight stores was finished by the spring of 1958.

Photo from the James Detore Archive/UVM Silver Special Collections.

The ten store extension of the Essex Junction Shopping Center just after their grand opening in 1958. Original tenants that are visible include Vermont Cleansing, Ben Franklin, Greenfield Furniture, Knight's Pharmacy (Rexall), and a Grand Union Supermarket.

An extension with more stores was added within the year. Like on North Avenue, the anchor stores were Grand Union and Ben Franklin. Other original tenants included a bakery, furniture store, cleaner, a lunch counter and a drug store. Further mirroring North Avenue, a bowling alley was added in a separate building, as was a gas station.

Back at North Avenue, at the Ethan Allen Shopping Center a second building was added, bringing the store count to 16, and the parking lot was more than doubled to 600 spaces.

In 1959 Pomerleau and the Haukes opened a third shopping center, called the Mount Mansfield Shopping Center on Williston Road. It's also been referred to as the Green Mountain Shopping center. The center was located in a spot with a panoramic view of the aforementioned mountains, thus the name. But most people just identified it by the name of the main tenant, Gaynes.

Gaynes was a local discount department store which has been discussed in the Mazel's section previously. It was very unusual to have a retail anchor that was not a national, or at least regional chain. But Sid and Lou Mazel had built up a great reputation and name recognition during their many years as retailers on North Street. A First National grocery store, the largest First National in Vermont, was the other anchor.

This shopping center prospered immediately, largely due to the success achieved by Gaynes. A few years after this center opened, it became easily accessible to those traveling from outside the Burlington area, as a large, cloverleaf intersection was constructed off of Interstate 89, just a stone's throw

Photo from the Lilian Baker Carlisle Collection/UVM Silver Special Collections.

Cars lined up at Gaynes Shoppers World in the early 70s. Gaynes was the only locally owned retailer that served as an anchor store for any of the shopping centers in Chittenden County.

away. Two years after opening, Gaynes expanded to 55,000 square feet, nearly the size of rival discounter Grand Way, located one exit south of the cloverleaf.

In 1960 Tony Pomerleau began development of the fifth and final of the early shopping centers in the area. This time he was both the developer and the owner. He acquired a large property at the corner of Home Avenue and Shelburne Road, which had been occupied for a century by the Burlington Children's Home, formerly known as the Home for Destitute Children.

The Children's Home was relocated to a new building, and the old buildings on the Children's Home campus were demolished. Work began on what would be known as the Shelburne Road Shopping Center, later called the Shelburne Road Shopping Plaza.

In May of 1962 the first phase of the shopping center opened. The anchors were national chain W.T. Grant, which was enticed to relocate from its longtime location on Church Street. They occupied a 25,000 square foot space on the south end of the building. Another chain store, a Super Duper supermarket, was on the northern end. The small number of stores in between included a City Drug store, a laundromat, and a Top Value trading stamp redemption store. This was the first of three planned buildings for this shopping center, which were slated to include a 24 lane bowling alley, a 50 unit motel, and many more additional shops.

But all of the plans for the Shelburne Road Shopping Plaza went out the window once Sears and Roebuck, the nation's largest retailer, decided to leave Church Street for Shelburne Road. Sears had been downtown since the late 30s, and had persevered there through a massive fire in 1940 that wiped out their store only a couple of years after it opened. Downtown was still the only game in town then for large national retailers.

By the early 60s the area's new shopping centers were sending shock waves through the world of retailing in Chittenden County. The five shopping centers, all opened within eight years of each other, were thriving even beyond their developers' expectations. Each continued to expand after their initial opening, creating a desirable mix of store types, big and small, local and national, with a wide variety of merchandise. Their appeal was supplemented by non-shopping attractions, such as the bowling alleys.

All of this started to have a very serious impact on downtown Burlington, which had already lost Grants and Agel-Corman to the shopping centers. Now, not only would Church Street lose one of its major stores, but the new

Photo by Donald Weidenmayer, Vermont State Archives.

The first lineup of stores in the new Shelburne Road Shopping Center in 1962. Chain stores W.T. Grant and Super Duper were at each end, with a Top Value trading stamp redemption center, City Drug store, and Snowflake Laundry between them.

Sears store that would be opening on Shelburne Road would be something that was of a magnitude never seen before in Vermont. Its presence would greatly compound the problem of downtown stores losing sales to the shopping centers.

The new Sears that opened on March 24, 1965 was truly gigantic. It had 106,000 square feet of retail space, including 26,000 in its automotive center. The automotive center by itself was larger than the entire Sears store on Church Street. The Shelburne Road store had 49 departments, 22 more than Church Street. It featured 60,000 different items. If that wasn't sufficient, you could order from 140,000 items via their catalogue sales department. The store featured a coffee shop/luncheonette that seated 56. All of this was supported by a 49,000 foot warehouse on Bartlett's Bay Road in South Burlington. This Sears was like an entire shopping center itself, all in one building.

Taken all together, these five shopping centers had well over a hundred stores, some of them huge, and thousands of free parking spaces. They were easy to get to, and people flocked to them. In the early 60s iconic Church Street stores such as The Old Beehive, established in 1853, and Louis Pine (1898), started to close.

The five shopping centers were the vanguard of a revolution in local retail that continues to this day. All five are still going strong, although with a very different mix of stores. One bit of trivia: of all of the original tenants of

Photo from the Fred G. Hill Collection/ UVM Silver Special Collections.

The truly gigantic Sears store in the Shelburne Road Shopping Plaza stretches out to fill almost this entire photo. This is from the 70s after the initial façade was remodeled.

these five shopping centers, at this writing only one is still in business at its original location. That is the Quality Bake Shop, which has been in business continuously in the Essex Junction Shopping Center since moving there from Railroad Avenue in 1958.

Also, an interesting geographical quirk: The Seaway Shopping Center was in South Burlington, while the Shelburne Road Shopping Plaza, right across the street, was in Burlington.

Snack Bars and Drive-In Restaurants

Throughout the first half of the 20th century, dozens of soda fountains and lunch counters did business in downtown Burlington. It helped that both high schools, BHS and Cathedral, were each a short walk from Church Street, but busy shoppers wanting a quick bite made up most of the clientele. With the rise of the car culture, after the war, this new mobility that most enjoyed soon eroded that monopoly on snack bars and quick lunch joints that Burlington had enjoyed for so long.

Even if you couldn't drive or didn't own a car, chances are that you knew someone who did. All of a sudden Williston Road beyond Hinesburg Road, and Shelburne Road beyond the Children's Home, which had been considered remote regions, were just a quick hop away from Burlington in a car. Restauranteurs shifted gears accordingly, and numerous snack bars and drive-in restaurants opened on both of these busy thoroughfares during the 50s and 60s.

The A&W Restaurants

The A&W root beer stand on Shelburne Road, which opened in 1953, was one of the very first snack bars in Chittenden County to be established outside of the Burlington downtown core. A&W was a national chain based out of California. They specialized in root beer and floats, but also featured a full line of what would soon be known as fast food. Bill Eddy obtained a franchise, and opened his A&W drive-in at 1184 Shelburne Road.

The drive-in restaurant model meant that there was no seating. You drove up, parked, and a young lady came to take your order. In the early days, all of the wait staff at the A&W were female. While movies like to show car hops

The A&W drive-in on Shelburne Road in 1955. The Del Ray Motel is in the background. There is a remarkable story behind this photo. The picture was taken on June 15, 1955, which was the day the car hop on the right, Mary Bullis, got married. Right after the ceremony she walked her new husband, Mike Hurlbut to the train station and he headed for boot camp. She then proceeded to the A&W where she worked her shift. She had just graduated from Cathedral High School. Thanks to her daughter Mary Ellen Hurlbut Farrow for the photo and the story behind it.

A car hop waits on customers at the Williston Road A&W in this photo from 1955. The tray hanging from the car window where the food was placed can clearly be seen. Author's Collection.

on roller skates, I don't believe any of the drive-in restaurants in this area featured them. When the food was ready, you rolled your car window part way down and a specially designed tray was clipped to the window. The driver passed the food to his passengers and everyone munched away in the car. No need to worry about getting a table as long as there was a parking space available.

This new dining experience was an instant hit. America's love affair with the automobile was just hitting Chittenden County, and the drive-in restaurant was one of the many manifestations of that sea change in American life.

In addition to in car dining, you could just take the food and go elsewhere to eat it. A&W offered gallons of root beer in glass jugs and quarts in waxed cardboard cones, designed to be taken home. The restaurants were seasonal since they had no provision for indoor dining.

The first A&W in the area was such a hit that in 1955 Bill Eddy opened a second one at 1225 Williston Road. Then in 1959 he opened the A&W "Walk-In" restaurant on the corner of Church and College. He leased the space on the corner long occupied by the A. Schulte tobacconist shop. The Walk-In had a very distinctive double horseshoe counter that undulated across the space, fitting a lot of stools into a relatively small area.

Photo from the James Detore Archive/UVM Special Collections.

The A&W Walk-In at the corner of Church and College in 1965. Bracketed on both sides by the classic black glass storefronts of Abraham's, the photo gives a great view of the Art Deco enameled steel panels that conceal the 1820s Federal style brick building beneath. It's one of the oldest on Church Street.

Shortly after the walk-in opened, a fourth A&W, another drive-in, opened in Essex Junction on Pearl Street, Alfred Perrota was the initial franchisee.

But by the early 60s Bill Eddy and Alfred Perrotta were out of the picture. Bill Turnbaugh had bought the Williston Road and Essex Junction's drive-ins, and Bill and Pericles Maglaris bought Shelburne Road and designated it as the M&M A&W Drive-In (Maglaris & Maglaris). Eddy sold the downtown Walk-In to Frank Goldstein.

The A&Ws prospered through the 50s and 60s. The M&M A&W became a popular hangout for Rice High School students after games. But as more and more burger and pizza joints sprouted up on both Shelburne Road and Williston Road throughout the 60s, the landscape changed radically. While the A&Ws enjoyed little competition in their early years, they soon were confronted by numerous competitors, both local and national. Eventually all four outlets went out of business. Like Woolworth's, despite being part of a national chain, Chittenden County's A&Ws continue to evoke warm memories for those who patronized them.

One interesting note is that when the Williston Road A&W closed in 1969, it was replaced by Vermont's first McDonalds.

The University of Vermont Dairy Bar

The cows that provided milk for the UVM dairy bar could be seen grazing outside its windows when it opened in 1950. Located in the newly constructed Carrigan Dairy Science building, the Dairy Bar was set up as a non-profit under the supervision of a recent UVM graduate named Henry Atherton. It was a small setup, with limited offerings of ice cream, cottage cheese, and yogurt. It replaced a small dairy products store in Morrill Hall.

People enjoying UVM ice cream in cones from the UVM Dairy Bar. The locally produced dairy treats from the university's own cows were popular with locals and students for decades. 1992 photo from Vermont Quarterly/UVM Silver Special Collections.

The Dairy Bar was an immediate hit. Its prices were quite low as it didn't have the expenses of a downtown ice cream parlor. And its location made it the first option for generations of students wanting a milk shake or cone after a hard day of classes. It became one of the most popular aspects of the UVM campus for both students and locals, an early version of the "buy local" phenomenon.

By the 1980s things began to change. Competition from several Ben and Jerry's campus scoop shops ended the Dairy Bar's former advantage of location. Its limited flavor menu seemed old fashioned compared to Ben and Jerry's inventive offerings. The small size of the Dairy Bar (9 stools) limited its ability to increase income. It began to lose thousands per year. Mary Dion, who had run the Dairy Bar since the early days, retired in 1991. Marriott, the school's food service provider, took over management of the Dairy Bar. They refurbished the facility and expanded the menu. The Dairy Bar soldiered on for a few years, but finally closed in 1995. Its former home, the Carrigan building, was demolished in 2006 to make way for the new Davis Center, which features a Ben and Jerry's.

Whether it was the quality of the ice cream, the prices, the unique nature of the Dairy Bar, or all three, the UVM Dairy Bar remains a nostalgic memory for many area residents and former students.

The Lure

Most locals who grew up in the 60s have great memories of the Lure on Williston Road. It was where many headed after big games to fuel up on inexpensive burgers, shakes, and hand-cut fries. Some places seem to stand out in people's memories from their high school days, and certainly the Lure was in that category.

The place was quite small, with glass walls. It had a large lot with many spaces, typical of 60s drive-in restaurants. It was located at 1200 Williston Road, right next to the Alpine Shop.

In addition to eating at the Lure, many high schoolers worked there as well. For a while the Hullabaloo teen dance club was right behind it, providing another reason for kids to flock there.

The Lure building and lot were owned by Mr. and Mrs. Angelo Rorris, but their nephew Nectar ran the restaurant. A large sign in front advertised 15¢ hamburgers when the Lure opened in 1961. Those low cost burgers, along with tasty fries and thick shakes were irresistible to local kids.

In 1968 when McDonalds announced plans to open directly across the street from the Lure, Mrs. Rorris hired a lawyer to try to block the national chain from opening. That attempt was unsuccessful, and McDonald's opened across from the Lure at 1225 Williston Road in 1969. In 1973 the Lure was demolished and became the site of a Burger King. The Rorrises maintained ownership of the former Lure property and became Burger King's landlords. So rather than have to take on McDonald's themselves, they let Burger King do that, and collected rent checks from them as long as they stayed in the fight.

Although the Lure was only in business for about a dozen years, it has an outsize place in many people's memories of their high school years, myself included.

Proprietor Nectar Rorris went on to run another, much longer lasting Burlington restaurant, Nectar's, on Main Street.

The Lure, at 1200 Williston Road, was a popular high school hangout in the 60s. It's pictured here in a rare color photo.

Carrol's

Carrol's was a regional chain of drive-in restaurants featuring low cost burgers, shakes, and fries. They came to Burlington in 1967, and to make way for the restaurant, one of the oldest homes in South Burlington was demolished. The large 164-year-old home and carriage house was surrounded by mature elms and locust trees, and all of this was cleared. The location was on the east side of Shelburne Road, two doors south of Proctor Avenue. It was only a few steps from the Burlington city line, but Carrol's was in South Burlington. The restaurant was very popular with south-enders, especially students from nearby Rice Memorial High School.

The building featured a very futuristic design. It incorporated two very modern answers to McDonald's golden arches. Carrol's featured two very angular V-shaped installations trimmed with aluminum and blue glass panels. In most Carrol's restaurants these installations were on either side of the building, but in South Burlington the building extended well beyond each of the Vees. That was because unlike most Carrol's, which had car hop service, city officials had ruled that no food served at the South Burlington location was to be consumed in cars. For this reason a larger dining area needed to be created at the Shelburne Road Carrol's.

Carrol's traditional color scheme was red, white and blue. In another concession to local sensibilities, the area that would normally be red was mandated by city officials to be brick to better blend in with the neighborhood.

Carrol's signature menu item was called the Club Burger, but they seem to be mostly remembered for their series of giveaway drinking glasses featuring Looney Tunes cartoon characters such as Bugs Bunny, Tweety Bird, and Yosemite Sam.

Carrol's seems to be better remembered than many of the chain restaurants that came and went fairly quickly in the area, such as Arthur Treacher's, Lums and Shakey's Pizza. Some say that's because Carrol's food was better, but in my opinion it's because of those Looney Toons glasses. Back in the 70s you'd be hard pressed to find anyone that didn't have a least a few of them at home.

Carrol's opened on Shelburne Road in 1968, and closed in 1977.

Carrol's Shelburne Road restaurant in this architect's drawing that was submitted to South Burlington officials. Two available photos of Carrol's were not of sufficient quality, so I reluctantly went with a drawing. But it shows the restaurant well, including the expanded dining area and the brick façade that city officials required. Photo from South Burlington Planning and Zoning.

Carrol's also operated a chain of movie theaters, and one of those opened in Burlington in 1971, Carrol's Plaza 1&2, which was on Dorset Street.

The Carrol's restaurants are long gone. The last one closed in the 80s. But Carrol's still exists as a corporation, operating over 1,000 Burger King and Popeye's locations.

Seward's

Seward's expanded north from their Rutland base in 1962, opening their first Chittenden County restaurant in 1962 at the southern end of the new Seaway Shopping Center on Shelburne Road. Seward's was a longtime dairy in Rutland, and their restaurants emphasized dairy desserts such as milk shakes and ice cream, along with regular meal options. In 1969 they opened their second location in the new Pinewood Shopping Center in Essex. A few years later a third location opened in Burlington at the corner of St. Paul and Main, the longtime location of Valade's.

By the early 80s they were all gone, although I don't have specifics on when each closed. The Shelburne Road Seward's was popular with families and high schoolers. It was mainly a sit-down restaurant, although they also had a takeout window that did brisk business. Seward's featured unique concoctions such as their take on the milk shake, called the "Awful Awful" (awful big and awful good). They also featured a "Pig's Dinner", which was basically a banana spilt on steroids. It was served in a trough and if you could eat an entire Pig's Dinner they gave you a medal (which was actually a pin). The Shelburne Road Seward's had by far the longest run of the three locations, about 20 years.

The south façade of Seward's Dairy Restaurant in the Seaway Shopping Center is pictured in this image. The signage is a bit unusual, with the name in small letters, and "Restaurant" capitalized. The main entrance was around the corner, this side was for take out only. Photo from the Lilian Baker Carlisle Collection/UVM Silver Special Collections.

The Dairy Queen

For over 50 years the Dairy Queen was a favorite warm weather spot in the heart of Burlington's Old North End. In 1951 a small DQ creemee stand opened at 237 North Winooski Avenue. The opening of the Dairy Queen was one of the welcome signs that winter was finally over. It was another of those national chains that locals loved. The Burlington Dairy Queen was unusual not only because it opened before any of the many snack bars that sprouted later out in the suburbs, but also because it was situated in the Old North End, a location that wasn't used to getting a bonus like this.

At some point the small stand was expanded and modernized, with a barn like portion on one end, creemee windows, and a flat topped portion with the brazier and seating. A distinctive red roof topped off the look. People would line up for creemees at the stand, and since creemees don't travel well, other offerings such as Dilly Bars, Blizzards and Mr. Mistys were available to be taken back to those waiting at home.

There were three other Dairy Queens in Chittenden County in the 80s. One was in the former Red Barn snack bar at 1087 Williston Road, another was in Dorset Square on Dorset Street, and the third was in Colchester. Even well after 2000 a DQ operated in the University Mall. But the one on North Winooski Avenue was the oldest, biggest, longest lasting and most memorable of them all.

The Burlington Dairy Queen closed around 2006, and was operated for a time as QTee's. The building was demolished in 2014.

Burlington Free Press photo.

The North Winooski Avenue Dairy Queen at its peak, after it was dramatically expanded and offered "Brazier" service. It was a very rare example of a national snack bar chain with a location in the Old North End of Burlington.

When this DQ closed, Vermont became the only state without a Dairy Queen. Every summer the chain holds a free creemee day, and they set up a small stand in Montpelier so they can say they are pumping creemees in all fifty states.

Nourse's

Nourse's was a favorite summer spot in Mallett's Bay for about 20 years from the mid 30s to 1954. It was located on the other side of the bay from perennial favorites Bayside and Sadie's.

In 1934 George Nourse took over an existing store and sandwich shop and converted it to a snack bar specializing in toasted hot dogs. He renamed the former Sunset Sandwich Shop as Nourse's Place. It was a hot dog stand, with no sit down dining. You got your food and went to the car to eat, or more likely to the beach behind Nourse's. The venture was very successful, and by the early 40s he had opened a second location on Main Street in Burlington across from Memorial Auditorium.

In 1948 he constructed a new, larger Nourse's right next to the original stand. The new restaurant was a huge upgrade from the old hot dog stand as it featured a dining room and a modern interior. It was brightly lit, with a huge neon sign on top. Both old and new buildings featured beautiful views of Mallett's Bay for diners to enjoy.

Mr. Nourse had started Nourse's Place when he was 55 years old, and after running it for 20 years, he passed away in 1954. His widow repeatedly tried to sell the business, but Nourse's Place did not survive the loss of its founder.

Photo from the James Detore Archive/UVM Silver Special Collections.

Nourse's signs glow in this night time photo taken right after their new building at the right opened in 1948. The old hot dog stand can be seen at the left.

For many years after Nourse's closed, the beach there continued to be referred to as Nourse's Beach, and the former location of Nourse's, where Bay Road turns into Lakeshore Drive, continues to be referred to as Nourse's Corner.

Sadie's

In 1943 Sadie and Tom Raymond of Winooski opened Sadie's snack bar in Malletts Bay, right next to Clarey's Bayside. That same year Bernie Kriesel moved his family to Burlington. He had joined the World of Mirth carnival right after graduating from high school in Syracuse, playing trumpet in the carnival's swing band. While on the carnival circuit he encountered and fell in love with Vermont, and determined to find a way to move there. After leaving the carnival he had gone to work for Bell Aircraft in Buffalo, and when the war started and Bell opened a plant in Burlington, he saw his chance. He took a transfer to the Burlington plant on Lakeside Avenue, which was hiring hundreds of workers as they rapidly ramped up to start production.

It would take 25 years, but Sadie's and Bernie's paths would later cross in a significant way.

Sadie's started as a very small wooden building with no seating. Eventually the Raymonds expanded the snack bar, adding a kitchen and later a dining room onto the back. Sadie was famous for her hand-cut French fries, and everything that was prepared at the snack bar was made from scratch. She ran the place with military like precision, having automatic timers for everything so that workers knew exactly when to take the fries out of the oil for example.

Sadie's was seasonal, with the opening targeted for Easter weekend, and closing right after Labor Day. So the Raymonds tried to maximize their income during the roughly four months that they were open. Sadie's often stayed open very late to take advantage of the hungry crowds that would stream there as one of the two drive-in movie theaters in the Bay let out. On occasions when there were more than two features, Sadie's sometimes wouldn't close until three or four in the morning.

Finally, in 1967, after running Sadie's for nearly 25 years, the Raymonds were ready to ease off and decided to sell Sadie's. Meanwhile, Bernie Kriesel had moved to Sears on Church Street after Bell Aircraft closed their wartime plant in Burlington. He later went to work for Champlain Valley

Fruit as a salesman. He also resurrected his trumpet skills, moonlighting by playing in the orchestra aboard the steamboat Ticonderoga.

Learning that Sadie's was for sale, he bought the business. Under the terms of the sale, Kreisel agreed that nothing would be changed for at least five years: the food prep, the name, nothing would be different from when Sadie's was run by Sadie Raymond. No doubt Bernie Kriesel knew that it would be business malpractice to change the name of a local icon. As for the food, why mess with success? Kriesel not only kept all of Sadie's methods in place for the required five years (except for adding menu items) he kept everything the same as it was under Sadie for the entire time he ran the snack bar. Sadie often stopped by in the years after the sale, and was very pleased to see how the place was being operated.

Under Bernie Kriesel Sadie's became a true family operation. His children and grandchildren worked at Sadie's for years, the kids starting work as soon as school was done for the year. Dean LaMothe, Bernie's grandson, worked there for years, and loved Sadie's so much that he named his daughter Sadie. Under Kriesel, Sadie's closed much earlier than when Sadie ran it, shutting down at 11:00, and in the later years, at 10:00. Peeling mountains of potatoes for French fries was a big part of working at Sadie's. The family would have potato peeling competitions when they would get together for family picnics and other gatherings. The winner would proudly look down on the vanquished fellow family peelers.

Under Kriesel, pizza burgers were introduced to the Burlington area, and the family indicated that Sadie's was the first local snack bar to feature black raspberry creemees. A cotton candy machine was added. Bernie wanted to start breakfast service at Sadie's but Sadie talked him out of it.

In 1987 Sadie's was still prospering. After 45 summers of serving up food at the Bay, Sadie's had become a beloved part of everyone's summer. The lease on the land that Sadie's sat on was coming to an end, but no one dreamed that getting it extended once again would be a problem. But it did turn out to be a problem, a big problem.

The owner of the land informed Bernie that his lease would not be renewed, and that he must vacate. Stunned by this news, Bernie tried to convince his landlord that he needed a bit more time to dispose of his equipment and to wind down Sadie's in an orderly fashion. This fell on deaf ears. The landlord told Bernie that he needed to vacate the premises immediately after the lease ran out as he had plans to construct a bank branch on the site.

So Sadie's was torn down, and the debris hauled away. That bank was never built, and nearly 40 years later, the land where Sadie's once sat remains a vacant lot.

Author's Collection.

Sadie's snack bar in Malletts Bay. A fun part of everyone's summer for decades, it was located next to Clarey's Bayside.

Charlie's Red Hots

Sam Costopoulos, who was known as Charlie, started selling red hots on Church Street in 1941 after working in the restaurant business downtown for 20 years. After working in other people's restaurants, by 1935 he finally decided to go out on his own, operating the Yum Yum Pastry Lunch at 63 Church Street. A short mention in 1935 indicates that his Yum Yum Lunch also featured Texas hot dogs, the only place in the state where they were available. By 1940 Yum Yum Lunch moved up Church Street to the Royal Grill of the New Sherwood Hotel, and Charlie moved down Church Street to number 179, a very narrow storefront across from the old Post Office building, that could truly be described as a hole in the wall. Coincidentally, the previous occupant had been Charlie's Chop Suey Cottage, a Chinese restaurant run by a man named Charlie Joe.

A 1941 ad for Charlie's new restaurant has no mention of Red Hots. The name of the place was Charlie's Restaurant, and the ad showcased Texas and Michigan hot dogs. The first mention of the restaurant as Charlie's Red Hots was in 1943. In photos taken shortly after the name change, painted signage on the front window reads "Charlie's Texas and Michigan Red Hots." The words "Red Hots" were in large letters. A neon sign hanging above the store showed an image of Charlie surrounded by the words "Charlie's Red Hots." A local institution had been born.

It's a testament to the popularity of Charlie's that after he started selling Red Hots, he never advertised again. It was not uncommon for a popular small business, especially one with low overhead, to not bother with advertisements. If people were flocking to the place, ads were seen as a needless expense. And Charlie's certainly became popular. So much so that by the early 50s they had opened a second location on the way to Mallett's Bay, just across the Heineberg Bridge.

Charlie would hang a photo behind the counter of the champion Red Hot eater. Once someone had consumed more Red Hots than the champ, their photo would take the place of the dethroned eater.

Photo from the James Detore Archive/UVM Special Collections.

"Charlie" (Sam Costopoulos) ladles out his signature hot sauce in the tiny kitchen area of his Church Street hot dog stand.

Charlie prepared hot dogs in a tiny area in the front of the restaurant. Customers sat at a counter. People would often stop for a minute to watch him at work. A sign on the wall said, "After you eat, give your seat to the next customer and we'll all be happy."

Charlie's son George started working at Charlie's when he was in the sixth grade. Eventually George took over the business.

According to the obituary of George Costopoulos, the Church Street Charlie's Red Hots closed in 1986, and George and his wife continued to run the Mallett's Bay location until his retirement in 1997.

People are still passionate about Charlie's Red Hot sauce, and tales of the colorful proprietors abound.

The Dilly Wagon

The Dilly Wagon wasn't a national chain, but there were several of them in the region, including two in Chittenden County. The concept was conceived by Charles Weinstein of Potsdam, New York. It was based on his so-called Dilly Sauce, a mayonnaise based sauce flavored with dill that also had something added for heat. It was said to go equally well with meat or fish. The other part of his concept was designing his restaurants to look like Conestoga covered wagons. Weinstein opened his first "It's a Dilly" restaurant in his home town of Potsdam in May of 1961. Three others followed within a few months, one of which was in South Burlington.

That first Dilly Wagon in Chittenden County was opened by franchisee Mrs. Ken Bissonette. She opened her restaurant in July of 1961 at 1907 Williston Road. It got the full Conestoga treatment and it certainly caught people's eye. The wagon was very eye catching from the road, and along with the Dutch Mill on Shelburne Road, the Dilly Wagon's Conestoga was probably the most significant piece of novelty, or vernacular roadside architecture ever to appear in Chittenden County. The menu included dilly burgers (with dilly sauce), dilly dogs, dilly snacks, fried chicken, shrimp in a basket, etc.

Weinstein advertised in the Burlington Free Press to solicit additional franchises for his "It's a Dilly Enterprises." You could open a franchise with or without the signature Conestoga wagon. The franchise fee nearly doubled if it included the wagon, but as a piece of roadside art/architecture and as a way to get noticed, that extra money seemed to be very well spent by those who did.

Photo from California Crazy: Roadside Vernacular Architecture and Beyond.

An example of the Dilly Wagon's eye-catching Conestoga wagon. Only one very poor quality photo of the Williston Road Dilly Wagon was available, but this one of the Rutland Dilly Wagon gives a great picture of what their signature Conestoga on Williston Road looked like.

In 1968 Vermont Air National Guard pilots Richard Corley and Jan Rozendaal, bought the Ethan Allen Lanes and A.J.'s Lounge at the Ethan Allen Shopping Center on North Avenue. They converted A.J.'s into the area's second Dilly Wagon. This one did not have the Conestoga Wagon since it was located in a shopping center, but it featured rustic western décor in keeping with Weinstein's theme. That same year they also bought the Williston Road Dilly Wagon.

In June of 1971 the Conestoga wagon on Williston Road suffered considerable damage in a fire. It did not re-open. As Rozendaal put it "By then the big boys had moved in and put us out of business", referring to the national fast food chains that were popping up in the area.

But to this day, despite its short run, the Dilly Wagon is one of the best-remembered of the area snack bars, and it's largely because of that Conestoga wagon, which sadly, did not survive after the Dilly Wagon closed.

Traditional Restaurants

By "traditional" I mean a sit-down restaurant as opposed to a drive-in. I need to add this clarification because the first two restaurants discussed in this section were anything but traditional in every other sense of the word.

The Harbor Hideaway

The Harbor Hideaway was built in the 40s by local optometrist Wallace White, who owned a gun shop next door. It was located on Shelburne Road, just north of the turn for Bay Road.

He kept adding to it by incorporating neighboring structures into the restaurant. It was packed with all sorts of weird stuff inside, making for a unique, if sometimes creepy, dining experience. A skeleton in a coffin was just one of the many bizarre items to be found there. Drums hung from the ceiling and numerous swords and muskets adorned the walls. You might eat your dinner under the gaze of a cigar store Indian. I remember eating there one night and above our table was a painting of a skull with the words "Vanity of Vanities, All is Vanity" (from Ecclesiastes). Whether you saw this as weird and wacky or were creeped out by it depended on your point of view. Interiors varied from a multi-colored room that was green, red and yellow, to a pink themed dining room, and one with very dark Victorian style wallpaper. There was a naval gun mounted outside the front entrance.

Walter White sold the Harbor Hideaway in 1983 after a long, successful run in the area dining scene. The buyer was John Ondovchik, who ran the restaurant for a few more years before closing it. He held on to the property, thinking that at some point he would re-open the restaurant, but this never happened. During all those years after it closed, the old restaurant became a crumbling eyesore on busy Shelburne Road. Ondovchik died in the summer of 2012, and the family soon sold the building along with 13 acres to the DuBrul family. They quickly demolished the building and used the land to expand their Automaster car dealership.

The Harbor Hideaway was unique, and no matter what you thought of it, if you ever ate there, you never forgot it.

The colorful exterior of the Harbor Hide-Away is seen in this internet postcard view.

Carbur's

Carbur's was founded in 1974. The name was a combination of the founder's names, Carl Capra and Burr Vail. They were classmates at the Cornell Hotel Management School. While dining at a DC eatery that featured items named for Washington politicians, they decided that this was something they could do, and headed for Vail's native state of Vermont.

Their Burlington location was at 119 St. Paul Street, originally built as the Burlington Elks Lodge. Eventually there were four other Carbur's locations; in Maine, Massachusetts and Plattsburgh, New York. Carbur's was famous for their humorous and ridiculously lengthy menu, which ran to over 25 pages. It featured 100 sandwich options, and many other dishes and desserts unique to Carbur's. The plethora of choices carried over to their beer menu, dubbed "Around the World in 80 Beers," which highlighted local and international brews.

Any restaurant efficiency expert would have told them that their menu was far too big, but the customers loved it. It was chock full of irreverent humor and painful puns: The Rare LeClair, named for local NHL star John LeClair. The Big Joe Burrito, for legendary Burlington saxophone player Big Joe Burrell. Leonardo DiCapicola, Shiitake Happens, Lady Chatterly's Liver, Phisherman's Platter. You get the idea. The menu was so entertaining that many diners would take one home with them after their meal. Carbur's posted a notice begging customers not to take the menus, which they finally offered for sale at a nominal price.

Occasionally Carbur's naughty menu items ruffled feathers, like when the National Organization for Women called for a boycott of their Mae West "Turkey Bosom" sandwich. Vail was unbowed. Rather than succumb to the pressure, he added the tag line "The only sandwich boycotted by N.O.W.," to the Mae West entry on the menu.

The menu was only part of the fun, as anyone who ordered the five-decker Queen City Special found out when the sandwich was delivered followed by a parade of waiters banging pots and pans.

But Carbur's also put out excellent food, making most items from scratch. This combination of fun and great food quickly proved to be a winner with area diners. The menu was updated on a regular basis to keep things fresh.

Photo from Vermont Business Digest magazine/ UVM Silver Special Collections.

The genius behind Carbur's, Burr Vail, is seen at the front door of his eccentric and eclectic restaurant.

Carl Capra died in 1985 and Vail continued running Carbur's for another 14 years. In 1999 he sold it to an experienced restaurant operator, Andy Golbert. He made several changes, including reducing the size of the menu.

The loss of Burr Vail's leadership and style proved to be critical. After running Carbur's for only 18 months, Golbert quietly put Carbur's up for sale. Finding no takers, he closed Carbur's in June of 2001. After 27 years in Burlington, Carbur's magical run in Burlington was over.

The Hi Hat

The Hi Hat originated on Church Street as the Marathon Restaurant in 1934. It was started by Catherine and Peter Marchacos of Burlington, and the Marathon was selected as the winning choice in a naming contest run by the family. No doubt the name was a nod to the family's Greek ancestry.

But the Marathon name did not last long. In 1937 the family renovated the Marathon and renamed it the Hi Hat. Early in 1942, the proprietor of the Hi Hat was Louis Marchacos. His father Peter had died in 1940. Louis was a star athlete at Burlington High School, the leader of the so called Wonder Team, the basketball team that was 24-1 and finished second in the New England tournament, besting schools from much bigger cities before falling in the finals.

After graduating, Louis and some fellow BHS alums continued to dominate local amateur basketball circles on their team known as the Hi Hats. But in February of 1943 Louis entered the service as a gunner on a bomber. Just six weeks after going overseas, in May of 1944, he and the other nine members of his crew were killed in Italy when their bomber crashed just 30 miles after taking off from their base.

The family and many others in the city were devastated. A tribute to Louis would hang on the wall of the Hi Hat for years afterward. But the family carried on, Catherine running the Hi Hat as it became one of Burlington's most popular restaurants. The place was fairly small, with seating limited to 15 booths. A small bar was located at the rear.

In 1946 Catherine gave up running the Hi Hat in favor of her daughter Chrysanthe, known as Sadie, and her husband, Nick Contos. In 1952 the couple gave the Hi Hat a complete makeover: new booths, a bar, a new ceiling and air conditioning. The storefront was redone in large panels of Carrara black glass. Large plate glass windows were on either side of the entrance, over which was installed a beautiful Art Deco style neon sign.

But the Hi Hat only stayed in this renovated space for eight years. By this point many of the area's restaurants were also featuring live music, either vocalists or bands, often with dancing available. The line between restaurants and night clubs was becoming blurred. But the Hi Hat did not have enough space to engage in this new trend. Nick Contos remedied that when he moved the Hi Hat into a much larger space at 186 Main Street in 1960. This space had been occupied for years by the Burlington Federal Savings and Loan, who had just moved to their new building on the corner of Bank and St. Paul Streets.

The new Hi Hat would be much more than a restaurant. On the ground floor was the restaurant and a cocktail lounge with a large horseshoe shaped bar. The cocktail lounge featured a dance floor as wells as booths and tables. It would soon become a popular night spot featuring bands and vocalists, a "supper club" in the parlance of those days.

The top floor, which was reached by a curving staircase, was mostly

Photo from the James Detore Archive/UVM Silver Special Collections.

The Hi Hat, long regarded as one of Burlington's best restaurants, after its façade was modernized. The Star restaurant is to the left. The Hi Hat would later move around the corner to Main Street and would be succeeded by Nectar's.

devoted to banquet space, along with a smaller cocktail lounge. All together, the new Hi Hat could accommodate 400 people.

The exterior was redone in a modern style with a large zig-zag style metal canopy over the front entrance. Neon was used extensively, in the overhead "Hi Hat" sign over the front door and the word "Restaurant" in block letters on one side and "Lounge" in flowing script on the other.

The Hi Hat had already established a reputation as one of the best restaurants in the area. The new Hi Hat became a favorite for private parties, wedding receptions, business lunches, and so forth. Meanwhile, its two lounges made it a popular night spot, with live music and dancing most nights. In 1975 Nick and Sadie Contos retired. The Hi Hat was sold and became Nectar's, which has become a Burlington institution in its own right. Nectar's has been in business continuously since opening except for a brief interval when it was sold and the new owner renamed it McHat's, after his hat collection. A year later Nectar Rorris reacquired his restaurant and restored the Nectar's name. That stainless steel zig-zag canopy from the 1960 renovation is still there, the only legacy on the exterior from the Hi Hat days.

Bernardini's Cafe

Raphael (Ralph) Bernardini was born in Italy in 1878. He emigrated to America in 1901. In 1908 he opened a fruit store in Winooski, and in 1933 he opened Bernardini's Restaurant on Main Street in Winooski. Before he was done he would return to Italy 15 times to bring back other members of the Bernardini clan.

One of those family members, Ralph's brother Frank, started a grocery store at 35 Pearl Street in Burlington. The location was a large former dwelling on the corner of Pearl and South Champlain Street. The store occupied half of the ground floor. The other half was an apartment.

But in 1934 Frank got out of the grocery business and began Bernardini's Cafe at the location of his former grocery. Initially advertising plates of spaghetti for 25¢, within a few years Bernardini's was touting "The Best Spaghetti in town and a full line of American Food." Frank's wife Mary did the cooking, which by all accounts, was outstanding. One family member said that the turkey dinner at Bernardini's was the best she had ever tasted.

The place quickly became a popular spot for a good meal at a reasonable price, or to just stop in for a couple of beers.

Business was so good that in 1941 Bernardini expanded into the remainder of the ground floor, doubling their space to 1800 square feet. Kieslich Construction did the work, which included the erection of a large neon sign above the front door. By 1947 Frank's son Orero was managing Bernardini's, although Frank was still the owner.

In December of 1941, Bove's Restaurant had opened across Pearl Street, appealing to basically the same clientele as Bernardini's. But Bernardini's seemed to take the competition in stride. It helped that they were able to offer live music and dancing, something that the smaller Bove's could not.

By the early 60s the café was no longer operated by the Bernardini family. By that time it became well known that the restaurant sat in the urban renewal zone and was slated for demolition. Bernardini's last few years were marked by noise complaints, break ins, rowdiness, and trouble with local and state officials, signaling a change from the comfortable neighborhood restaurant/night spot that Bernardini's had been for most of its nearly four decades in existence. Bernardini's last year in business was in 1965. After that the café was demolished, one of the 124 buildings taken down for urban renewal.

Photo from the James Detore Archive/UVM Silver Special Collections.

Bernardini's Café at 35 Pearl Street after the restaurant was expanded to the entire ground floor and the large neon sign was installed.

The corner lot that was the site of Bernardini's remains vacant. It was included in the large parcel of land that the Burlington Square Mall developers swapped to St. Paul's Episcopal Parish in return for the site of their burned out Cathedral land on St. Paul Street. St. Paul's built their new cathedral on their newly acquired parcel, which also would come to include the Cathedral Square building. The old Bernardini's lot was part of the St. Paul's property that was left as open land.

The Sugar House

When the Hotel Vermont reached its 25th anniversary in 1936, the entire hotel was updated from the basement to the roof garden on top. The basement upgrade involved converting three storage rooms into what would become a popular Burlington night spot called The Sugar House.

The space was made over to resemble an old time Vermont sugaring operation from several generations ago. Beams from an old barn on the Winooski River that had been wrecked by the 1927 flood were salvaged and used throughout the new space. A couple from Massachusetts was hired to paint three large murals, two on the north and south walls showed sugaring scenes in snow covered woods. The third featured a sunset over Lake Champlain as seen from Burlington. In later years a huge stone fireplace replaced the mural on the south wall of the space. Items such as old sap buckets and ox yokes hung throughout the new tap room.

Completing the look was the trunk of a large old maple tree that was affixed to the St. Paul Street side of the building. An opening was cut

Photo from the James Detore Archive/UVM Silver Special Collections.

The interior of the Sugar House right after the renovation of the space was completed. Two of its three murals are visible in the image.

through the concrete wall, the tree trunk was installed, and a door was cut through the trunk to serve as the entrance to the Sugar House.

In 1943 the hotel commissioned Burlington architect Louis Newton to design a new entrance for the Sugar House. His new entrance featured the façade of an old sugar house, covered with weathered shingles. Its salt box style roof was topped by a stone chimney. Above its weathered wooden entry door hung a sign with the words "Sugar House" on it. Newton's entrance is still there today, but the old tree trunk entry was removed many years ago.

In the 50s the Sugar House started serving dinner. It was a popular spot for civic groups to hold their meetings. In the evenings Red Dower would hold forth on the organ, which was situated on the inside portion of that old tree trunk that was no longer used as the entrance. The huge mural of Lake Champlain behind the bar was wired with electric lights, with an electronic mechanism to control them to simulate a sunset over the lake. When a button was pushed, the sun in the scene would grow brighter, and the colors of the sky would change as the sun slowly set behind the mountains. The entire display took about five minutes, and was run several times per night "at the bartender's whim." When the electronic display ceased working, that was the end of the sunset show. Supposedly the thing was designed by some sort of electrical genius at General Electric, and after he died, no one knew how to fix his creation.

Photo from UVM Silver Special Collections.

This 1959 image shows the entrance designed by architect Louis Newton in the style of a weathered Vermont sugar shack. This photo is rare because you can also see the original entry door which was through a large tree trunk, which can be seen at the left.

The Sugar House was a popular Burlington night spot for dining or just having a few drinks during its 35 year run. But in 1970 it was announced that the Hotel Vermont would be converted into apartments. Richard Corley and Jan Rozendaal, who also owned the Dilly Wagon and Ethan Allen Lanes, took over the Sugar House, retaining the name and operating it as a restaurant. But that arrangement didn't last long. By the fall of 1971 What's Your Beef had moved into the old maple sugar themed space, bringing down the curtain on the Sugar House.

The Olde Board

After the Waubanakee golf club on Shelburne Road closed in 1947, Burlington developer Thomas Farrell acquired the golf course. His first project was to convert the old Waubanakee club house into a restaurant. Over a period of 12 years he had been gathering old wooden beams from century old Vermont barns. Even back in those days, Vermont farms were closing and their buildings falling into ruin. Farrell wanted to preserve as much as he could, and eventually he had beams and other pieces from 23 different barns, many gathered by ox and horse teams, as some of the abandoned barns were not accessible by truck. Added to that were the stones from numerous foundations of barns, inns and homesteads that were gathered and used to construct two enormous fireplaces at the restaurant Farrell was building. The entry door was 8 inches thick, and hung on massive old iron hinges. Hand hewn beams up to 20 x 20, and weathered boards up to 20 inches wide could be seen throughout the interior. Weathered wood from the Waubanakee clubhouse itself was repurposed as the exterior of the Olde Board. Only 20% of the old lumber gathered by Farrell was used in the construction.

Hand selected calf skins decorated the bar, and local craftsmen built the tables and chairs, as well as the unique chandeliers, which were made from apple tree branches. The result was a feast for the eyes and a celebration of old time Vermont. The Olde Board opened in the summer of 1948. It could accommodate 250, and the dining room could be divided into smaller areas for private events. The club portion sat 135 and featured an elevated dance floor.

The restaurant was located far back from the road, behind the Seaway Shopping Center that Farrell would eventually build on the old golf grounds.

The Olde Board quickly became a favorite spot for dining and events, as well as for entertainment at the club portion. After many successful years,

Farrell leased it to private operators. They ran two restaurants in the space: Pitcairn's, and HMS Bounty. The club portion was redesignated as the Yankee Trader Room. Eventually the firm operating the club fell behind in their payments, and the Olde Board closed in the summer of 1978. It re-opened later, and the restaurant lived on as Michael's and later New England House. The club portion morphed from Yankee Trader Room to Club New England. Club New England continued as a popular venue for live music for a number of years. Ads still mentioned the Olde Board, but in much smaller print than Club New England. Eventually the Olde Board was dropped entirely. The owner of Club New England ran into tax trouble, and the club closed in 1991.

Next came Bambino's (eventually Cheers-Bambino's), which opened as a sports bar, but featured everything from turkey dinner on Thanksgiving to ladies oil wrestling. They went out of business in 1999, and seem to have been the last occupant of the space.

The Olde Board was eventually demolished, and one can't help but wonder what happened to everything that Thomas Farrell so painstakingly gathered back in the 40s to make the Olde Board such a showplace.

Author's Collection

Seen in this post card view is the Olde Board Restaurant, Thomas Farrell's tribute to old time Vermont, which was located in the original clubhouse of the Wabanaukee Golf Course. Farrell bought the entire course to build his Seaway Shopping Center.

The Star Restaurant/The Lotus

The Star Restaurant opened as a restaurant serving diner style food in 1894. It had a very conspicuous location on Church Street, right across from City Hall. So it was one of the oldest restaurants in Burlington when three Chinese-Americans from Bangor, Maine purchased it in 1921. They started serving Chinese food at the Star, a first in Burlington, and likely the first ethnic food of any sort served in the city. The restaurant's large star shaped overhead neon sign advertising "American and Chinese" can be seen in many old photos of this block.

In 1947 Jimmy Young bought the Star and renamed it the Lotus. He was another Chinese immigrant, and had come to Burlington in 1935. He redecorated the restaurant with Chinese motifs throughout in keeping with its new name, from the mosaic tile floor to the bright red upholstery of the seats, topped off by the Chinese themed bar. Patrons ate in booths, and although Chinese food was emphasized, ads for the Lotus always mentioned that "superior" American food would continue to be served as well. You couldn't miss the new exterior, which was bright red with gold trim.

Jimmy Young was a meticulous restauranteur, but it seemed that he may

Photo from the James Detore Archive/UVM Silver Special Collections.

Jimmy Young sits at the bar of his newly renovated Lotus Restaurant. The restaurant was made over to reflect motifs, themes and colors reminiscent of his native China.

have overextended himself. In 1952 he assumed management of the Alps Café and Sea Grill, which had been in business for 25 years across Main Street from City Hall. He also was running a gift shop called the Lotus Treasure House, and managing the South Hero Inn. In 1955 his Lotus Corporation went into receivership. But somehow he emerged intact, and in 1962 he took over management of the Olde Board, and then in 1964 he purchased the South Hero Inn.

But in 1968 he suffered a fatal heart attack while playing shuffleboard at Chez Dufais on Pearl Street. He was only 61. The Lotus was purchased by a couple from New York City who ran it without changing much. In the mid 70s the name was changed to the Golden Dragon, which closed in the late 80s. Another Chinese restaurant, the Mandarin, then opened in the space.

Improbably, the Golden Dragon re-opened in 1997 after a ten year absence from their former Church Street space, but that re-incarnation was short lived.

Kohala Mauna

The Kohala Mauna was a Polynesian/Chinese restaurant at the corner of Swift Street and Shelburne Road. The proprietors were the Lee family from Massachusetts, who had been running a restaurant in Leominster, which they closed. They had no links to Chittenden County, but were looking around for a location to open another restaurant when a vacant building in South Burlington came to their attention.

The nearly new building had been built for Cobb's Restaurant, a chain whose franchise in South Burlington had an incredibly short run. Cobb's opened in December of 1968 and closed in September of 1969.

The Lees made some alterations, and Kohala Mauna opened in March of 1970. Their bright red roof was hard to miss as you drove by on Shelburne Road. The location was right off the 189 spur leading to interstate 89, so access was easy.

While Chinese food had been available locally for years, the Polynesian specialties they offered were unique, and a big hit. Maybe an even bigger hit were their exotic drink options, with colorful names such as the Suffering Bastard, the Zombie and the Scorpion Bowl. Cocktails were available in any color of the rainbow.

In 1975 the restaurant expanded their seating to keep up with their robust growth. An all you can eat buffet called Kim's Oriental Buffet was added in the 80s. Kim Lee was one of the owners.

Over the years, people asking for the recipes for food served at the Kohala Mauna were regularly seen in the Ask It Basket column of the Burlington Free Press. So the food was very popular.

But finally, after nearly 20 years in business, the Kohala Mauna ceased operation in 1989. The national chain Denny's, which had been operating out of the Champlain Mill, moved into the old Kohala Mauna space in 1990.

Photo from the Lilian Baker Carlisle Collection/UVM Silver Special Collections.

The Kohala Mauna, one of Chittenden County's more memorable restaurants, sat by the on ramp to interstate 89 in South Burlington. The Lee family ran it for 20 years.

Tortilla Flat

Tortilla Flat was another pioneer in bringing ethnic food to Chittenden County. When it opened in 1971 at 317 Riverside Avenue in Burlington, it was the first all-Mexican restaurant in Vermont. Back then, ethnic food choices in the area consisted of Italian or Chinese. Guacamole was unknown to most locals.

The owner was Max Powell Junior, whose father had operated both the Hotel Vermont and the Van Ness House Hotel in Burlington for many years. Powell Junior's Tortilla Flat Corp. was run by his sons and daughters. Son Dave Powell ran the Riverside Avenue restaurant that he patterned after Tortilla Flat, a famous Mexican eatery in Greenwich Village in New York City.

Locals ate up the tostadas, tacos, burritos, and other offerings served at Tortilla Flat. The combination platters offered a lot of food for a little money.

The converted house that Tortilla Flat occupied teetered on the edge of a steep bank that dropped down to the Winooski River. The house had barely escaped destruction when a gigantic washout of the bank occurred in 1955. The washout stopped abruptly at the west side of the building. Two garages associated with the house dropped around 20 feet straight down right next to 317 Riverside Avenue.

In later years the steep bank would continue to threaten the building, and in 1983 the restaurant had to close for two months when part of the kitchen separated from the main building. In 2004-2005 Riverside Avenue was rebuilt, and Tortilla Flat had to close for four months in 2005.

But that aside, Tortilla Flat was phenomenally successful. In 1980 the building housing the restaurant was enlarged with a 1200 square foot addition, adding 40 seats. Several more Tortilla Flats opened, in Stowe, Merrimack and Portsmouth, NH, and in Portland, ME.

Business continued to be excellent for years, as Tortilla Flat was regarded as *the* place to go in Chittenden County for Mexican Food. As Free Press food writer Candy Page described it, "Mexican comfort food, not particularly creative, but savory and filling."

So it came as a shock when Tortilla Flat closed abruptly on Monday, November 12, 2007. Not even the employees knew about the closing until they were told not to come in that day. Some said that it had never really

Author's Collection.

The sketch shows Tortilla Flat at 317 Riverside Avenue as it looked when it first opened, before it was expanded.

recovered from the long disruption caused by the road construction. Others said that it had been "coasting" for years, not advertising, or "reinventing" itself. So maybe after 36 years Tortilla Flat had just run its course.

The Arcadia Restaurant

The Arcadia Restaurant on Main Street was one of Burlington's most popular dining spots for over 40 years. It was founded in 1924 by William Maglaris, and took its name from the region in Greece where the Maglaris family came from. It was originally a narrow restaurant offering only counter service. In 1934 the size was more than doubled, with the addition of 16 booths, six tables, and a bar in the rear. The lunch counter was one of the largest in Burlington, with 20 stools. The interior had a very diner like appearance. From the start, business was brisk.

But by 1945 Maglaris had had enough. He had worked in the restaurant business for 40 years, 35 of which were in Burlington. After coming here from Chicago in 1910 he worked at Burlington's Boston Lunch, Star Restaurant, and Park Cafe before starting the Arcadia in 1924. The struggle to keep the Arcadia going during the food and manpower shortages caused by the war sealed his decision to retire.

The Arcadia was purchased by several people from Brattleboro. Andrew Moisis, a chef and husband of one of the new owners, would act as chef and manager. He was a very interesting character, among other things being a high level wrestler, a European champion from Cyprus.

In 1953 Mr. and Mrs. Moisis sold the Arcadia. The buyer was none other than William Maglaris, who bought back the restaurant he had founded 30 years earlier. At age 66 he hopped back into the restaurant business with both feet, operating not only the Arcadia, but also the A&W drive-in on Shelburne Road.

Maglaris conducted his third renovation of the Arcadia, always wanting to keep the place looking modern.

The restaurant had a great location next to the Flynn Theatre in the heart of downtown. It was popular with college students, shoppers, and movie goers who wanted a good quick meal at a reasonable price.

William Maglaris died in 1978, having been in the restaurant business in Burlington for over 60 years.

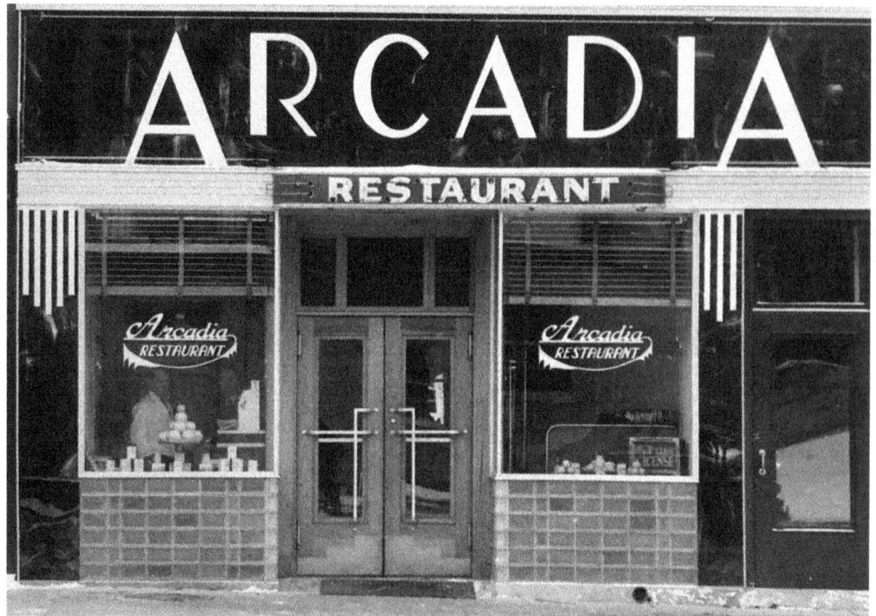

Photo from the James Detore Archive/UVM Silver Special Collections.

The Arcadia Restaurant, a Burlington icon for decades, stood on Main Street right next to the Flynn Theatre.

The Black Cat Café

The Black Cat opened in 1933. It was located right next to the State Theatre, in the same building, the Walker Block. Proprietor Charles Chantis had established a top notch reputation during his 20 years working at hotels and restaurants in the area.

The Black Cat was a great success from the start. The restaurant sat 150, but Chantis was constantly losing business because he had to turn away customers due to lack of available tables. So less than six months after opening, he did a major renovation, adding a second floor. This doubled his seating to 300, and he also added a private banquet room in the upstairs rear that could double as a performance space.

In 1939 a fire broke out in the basement of the Walker Block, and The Black Cat was so damaged in the fire that it was rendered a total loss (both floors). The adjacent State Theatre was nearly undamaged. The Black Cat fire was the worst in Burlington in 1939.

Chantis quickly rebuilt his successful restaurant. The fire was on November 12, and the fire debris was cleared and a new "modernistic" interior was completed in the remarkably short time of six weeks. The Black Cat re-opened on Christmas Eve.

By now the upstairs room had become very popular for banquets and private parties, and also for performances by various big city touring night club acts.

In 1948 the Black Cat was renovated yet again. The ground floor dining room was completely done over with modern touches such as indirect lighting, artificial palm trees, and palm leave themed wallpaper that gave the bar a tropical feel. A new cocktail lounge was added. But also during the makeover the footprint of the restaurant was cut in half as the entire second

Photo from the James Detore Archive/UVM Silver Special Collections.

The large neon sign and the canopy dominate the front of Charles Chantis' Black Cat Café in this 1948 photo. The Black Cat suffered major fire damage twice, but was rebuilt both times. A third fire and explosion destroyed the entire building.

floor was eliminated, suggesting that the night spot wasn't as successful as in earlier years. But from all appearances, through the 50s the Black Cat continued as one of Burlington's best places to go for dinner.

But trouble started in the early 60s, and in 1962 the IRS closed the Black Cat for non-payment of taxes. Later that year Chantis lost his restaurant as it was sold at auction by the IRS. Nicholas Zontas, owner of the Lincoln Inn, bought it.

The Black Cat remained in operation for another 15 years, but it's safe to say that it was no longer the renowned Burlington restaurant that it was under Charles Chantis. In their final years they featured yards of beer, beer served in a three foot tall glass propped up on a wooden stand. With the passage of time this is what most, including myself remember about the Black Cat. Its glory days were too far in the past.

The Black Cat and the State were both destroyed in a tragic explosion and fire resulting in loss of life on April 29, 1977.

The Park Café

Gus Poulos came to Burlington from Greece in 1905 and started his career in local restaurants at the Boston Lunch in 1908. In 1916 he purchased the Star Restaurant. After selling the Star in 1922, he and wife Winifred opened their Park Café and Sea Grill on November 3, 1923. It was located at 143 Main Street, next to where the Flynn Theatre would be built a few years later, and across the street from City Hall Park, thus the name.

The ad announcing their opening said "No Cold Storage Food Served." The freshness and quality of the food was emphasized from the start. The "Sea Grill" portion of their name indicated that sea food was their specialty. Ads indicated that they were the only sea grill in Burlington.

The Park quickly established a reputation as the best restaurant in town. The space was narrow but very deep, and three long rows of round tables extended from back to front. The bar and a small performance space were at the back of the room.

After running the restaurant for nearly 25 years, the Pouloses leased the space to Nick and Sara Pappas in 1947. At this point Gus Poulos was 65 years old, and had been operating restaurants in Burlington for 40 years.

The Pappases ran the Park for 15 years, upholding the excellent reputation that had been established by the Pouloses. In 1949 the Park made the annual Duncan Hines list of recommended American restaurants. Only 1% of eating establishments made that list, and the Park was the only one in Burlington so honored. It would regularly appear on the Duncan Hines and AAA recommended lists.

In 1962 the Pappas' 15 year lease at 143 Main Street was expiring. They then relocated the Park to a space that they had acquired a few years earlier at 139 Main Street, the site of their Gilded Cage cocktail lounge. To avoid any conflicts, they changed the name from the Park Café to the Park Restaurant. The new, larger space was renovated using striking red upholstery and walnut paneling and trim. The new Park Restaurant sat ninety for dinner, and incorporated the Gilded Cage cocktail lounge, which featured entertainment nightly. It had a small area sectioned off behind a giant bird cage for those seeking a bit more privacy. Also included was a room for private parties and banquets called the Cameo Room.

Photo from the L.L. McAllister Archive/UVM Silver Special Collections.

The Art Deco exterior of the Park Café shows how narrow it was, but it made up for that deficiency by being extremely deep. The Flynn Bowl was to the left.

The Park Café continued to prosper, but the Pappases had moved into other ventures, specifically Aunt Sara's Pancake House on Shelburne Road, which also housed Vermont's first Dunkin Donuts franchise. So in 1975 they closed the Park Restaurant, ending its run of over 50 years on Main Street. In 1984 they opened the Pappas Family Restaurant in the former Aunt Sara's building, but that restaurant was short-lived.

But the Park Café/Restaurant lives on in the memory of many locals, nearly 50 years after it closed. The quality of the meals is generally the first thing they mention.

Bove's

The terms iconic, legendary, and local institution get tossed around pretty freely, but if there was one area restaurant that merited all of those designations, it was Bove's Restaurant at 68 Pearl Street. Famously opened on the day Pearl Harbor was attacked, December 7, 1941, Bove's embarked on a memorable run in Burlington that lasted nearly 75 years.

Louis and Victoria Bove introduced many new Italian dishes to Burlington diners using family recipes. Some of the dishes were prepared in the small kitchen at the back of the restaurant, and others were prepared at the Bove's home.

The opening day ad was simple:

Open Today
Bove Restaurant
68 Pearl Street
Today Italian Food—Spaghetti and Pizza

Significantly, this is the first time pizza is mentioned in any ad for any restaurant in town. Bove's opened in a building that had previousy been one of six First National stores in Burlington. Once First National opened their supermarket on Pearl and South Union, they closed all six of their small stores. Bove's original restaurant featured large plate glass windows with a central door inset between them, all a carryover from the First National days. Above the entrance a neon sign hung from the building, with the word "Bove's" running vertically down the sign, and the word "Café" underneath.

That sign would hang from Bove's for the entire existence of the restaurant.

At some point, I'm not sure exactly when, the front was updated to an Art Deco look using black glass panels with white trim. That's the Bove's we all remember.

Bove's was a bit of a walk from downtown, but it was ideally situated to serve the numerous Italian-American families in the blocks just south of it in Burlington's Little Italy neighborhood.

The restaurant featured booths along both side walls as well as down the center. A small bar was at the back of the restaurant, and the very small kitchen was in the rear, behind the bar. A large juke box sat in front of the booths in the middle. The wallpaper featured scenes of gondoliers on the Grand Canal in Venice. What many liked about Bove's was that virtually none of this changed from the first day to the last. Fiore, "Babe" Bove, a constant presence in the restaurant after his father Louis died in 1946, joked that the only thing they ever changed was the light bulbs. He claimed his complete lack of cooking ability was the reason that he served as Bove's bartender and front man from the time he was 19 until he retired at age 65.

Press photo by Kevin Hurley.

Interior of Bove's Restaurant shortly before they closed for good. Burlington Free Press.

Bove's featured huge portions at reasonable prices. Although Italian food was the draw for most, they also had a wide selection of "American food." I remember when I had a much bigger appetite, I would order spaghetti with French fries and peas, and walk away stuffed.

Bove's was very popular with the area's many college students. At Bove's they could get a filling, tasty meal for very little cash. In the glory decades of the 50s through the 70s, long lines to get in were a regular feature. But they moved quickly, as the servers were attentive and the food came out fast. It seemed that no matter when you ate at Bove's, Babe was always there behind the bar, with a good word for everyone as they paid their bill.

If you didn't want to wait, you could order take out. You parked in the lot beside the restaurant and went to the kitchen door on the side. One order of spaghetti and meatballs was usually enough for two meals at home. Bove's pasta and sauce was excellent even when warmed over.

Eventually the wave crested, you no longer had to wait in line to get in. Things change. Finally, the third generation of Bove's decided that it was time to close down the restaurant. Bove's served its final meals on Pearl Street on December 23, 2015.

Alfonso's

Ralph and Carmela Cioffi were from Rutland, and both were children of Italian immigrants. Ralph was very familiar with Burlington from his days as a traveling salesman, and saw it as the "metropolis." He dreamed of moving his family there one day. That dream was realized in 1959 when 37-year-old Ralph and Carmela moved to the Queen City. Another dream of theirs was fulfilled when they opened Alfonso's Restaurant on the corner of Church and Main Streets shortly after relocating. Alfonso's was named after Carmela's maiden name.

Alfonso's occupied a building that had a long history, having been built originally as a Baptist church in the early 1860s. For many years the corner location had housed a restaurant, the Comeata Lunch, the Champlain Restaurant, and then the Alps Cafe from the late 20s until the mid 50s. Ralph and Carmella Cioffi carried on the tradition of restaurants on that corner when they opened Alfonso's. The exterior featured a classic art deco façade with six-sided windows in aluminum frames surrounded by Carrara glass in black and cream colors. That façade was installed in 1947 by the proprietors of the Alps Café, and was one of at least a dozen similar art deco facades in downtown Burlington. Above the storefront on Main Street Ralph Cioffi installed a sign that read "Alfonso's Italian Restaurant" in red and white neon.

The Alfonso's space was narrow but deep. Booths lined both the east and west walls, and a row of tables was in the middle. The tables featured red and white checked tablecloths, with a candle in an empty Chianti bottle to complete the Italian ambience. Each booth had an individual jukebox. In the early years there was a full service bar/lounge area where a woman named Gladys played the piano nightly. Eventually this was eliminated to create more seating.

The food was traditional Italian dishes such as spaghetti, pizza, ravioli, chicken cacciatore, etc. Like other area eateries serving ethnic food back then, Alfonso's also featured a full line of "American food", steaks, chops, fried chicken, and so forth. Like everyone else they offered ham at Easter and turkey on Thanksgiving.

Their location a few yards from Burlington's two biggest theaters made Alfonso's a natural choice for a post movie dinner or snack. Many locals judged Alfonso's Italian dishes as highly as Bove's, which was kind of the local standard for many years. Alfonso's also became a favorite dining spot for students at the local colleges. In those days there was no cafeteria service on Sundays at UVM, St. Michaels, Champlain or Trinity. It was well known that you could get a great meal at Alfonso's for $5.00, so hordes of students would descend on Alfonso's every Sunday to the point that long lines would form outside.

Alfonso's was a family operation, with four of the Cioffi's five children working there (the fifth was too young). Also pitching in were cousins, a brother-in-law, aunts, and others. When Ralph and Carmela went on vacation, Carmela's sister Mary came to Burlington and ran the restaurant. She had many years of experience in the restaurant industry, so Alfonso's didn't miss a beat when the Cioffis were away.

Ralph Cioffi was very active in sponsoring local sports teams, such as bowling, basketball and softball, as well as the Golden Gloves boxing tournament.

Alfonso's time in business was relatively short, just 13 years. The Cioffis sold Alfonso's in 1972. It continued on for a couple more years under another operator. A few years after selling Alfonso's, the Cioffis moved to Naples, Florida where they opened Alfonso's Italian Deli, which they ran for a few years.

Photo courtesy of Sharon Cioffi Joiner.

Alfonso's Art Deco front on Main Street, across from City Hall. The photo shows Alfonso's second sign.

The Lincoln Inn

The Lincoln Inn opened in Essex Junction in October of 1914. A residence dating back to the 1860s was renovated and expanded for conversion into a hotel at that time. It was located at the corner of Park and Maple Streets, and across Maple Street from the new hotel was Lincoln Park, named for President Lincoln. The first proprietor was Ira Lincoln, who leased the property after successfully running a hotel in Underhill for many years. So was the Lincoln Inn named for President Lincoln, or for Ira Lincoln? We may never know.

The new hotel was built in the Victorian style, and had verandas on both the Park Street and Maple Street sides. It featured large rooms, with or without baths, and had electricity, steam heat, and "as good water as can be found in Vermont." The inn was conveniently located a short walk from the railroad depot in Essex Junction, and at the intersection of several main roads, which we've all come to know as the "five corners."

Dinner was offered from its earliest days, but the main focus of the Lincoln Inn was providing room and board for guests, and offering meals for meetings, private parties, banquets and other gatherings held at the inn. As late as 1945, the inn was only open to the public for a brief time each day: Sunday dinners from 12:30 to 2:15, and every other day from 6:00 to 7:15.

This continued to be the focus through several different owners during the 40s and into the 50s, with traditional American food being the bill of fare. In 1953 Nicholas Zontas and William Coumes bought the inn. Right after assuming ownership they added a large banquet room seating 200 on the south side of the building. The veranda on the north side of the building was torn off and replaced by a coffee shop seating 70. But despite the Greek heritage of both men, the menu remained centered on traditional items like turkey dinners, lobster and the like. They sold the Lincoln Inn in 1958 to a couple from Colorado, but Nicholas Zontas would resurface again soon.

In 1964 the Lincoln Inn was sold again, this time to Mr. and Mrs.

Photo from the Penobscot Marine Museum.

The Lincoln Inn is seen in the mid 50s, after the large addition on the south side was completed, but before the veranda on the north side was removed.

Thomas Kourebanas. Thomas was the nephew of former owner Nicholas Zontas, who would be featured in the newspaper in the years immediately following as the inn's proprietor. Under their management, the Lincoln Inn not only continued to offer their very popular takes on American comfort food, but also began to feature traditional Greek dishes. For most of the 20th century, Chittenden County's small Greek community was responsible for the vast majority of the area's restaurants, diners, and even snack bars. Despite this, Greek dishes were not to be seen on their menus. Nor was there a Greek restaurant. Except for Chinese and Italian food, there just weren't any other ethnic food choices. That all started to change under the Kourebanas' management as the Lincoln Inn began to feature items such as spanakopita, Greek salad and desserts such as baklava.

The Kourbanases sold the Lincoln Inn in 1986. There followed a bitter

Photo from the James Detore Archive/UVM Silver Special Collections.

The interior of the Lincoln Inn Coffee Shop, which was added to the north side of the building in the mid 50s.

legal battle over the ownership of the property that dragged on for several years. The Kourebanas family reacquired the inn in 1992, but by then it was a restaurant in decline. Business was suffering and the place was looking run down. They closed the place for a major renovation that took the better part of the year. The word soon spread among locals who had feared that the Lincoln Inn would close, and business picked up quickly once word of the revitalized icon spread. The coffee shop became a popular spot for breakfast, and the main restaurant regained its former popularity.

Alex Kourebanas, Thomas' son, ran the inn until 2004. So it had been in his family for 40 years except for a few years in the 80s. But by 2004 the family wanted to sell the inn so that Thomas and Martha Kourebanas could retire. The national chain Walgreens wanted to buy the inn to demolish it and build one of their drug stores on the site. But brothers Alex and Bob McEwing, Essex Junction natives, stepped forward and bought the Lincoln Inn to save it from the wrecking ball.

The Lincoln Inn Restaurant remained in operation until 2005. After that the various spaces in the building have been leased by several restaurants and pubs. At this writing it houses the On Tap Bar and Grill and the El Gato Cantina.

Valade's Terminal Restaurant

In May of 1939 the bus terminal on St. Paul Street opened after a major renovation. In addition to the facelift the building got, one of the major changes was the opening of a new restaurant to serve travelers and workers. The proprietor was George Valade, who had been working at Henry's Diner. His sister Grace was married to Henry Couture, proprietor of Henry's. The previous restaurant at the terminal had been run for years by Charles Upton, who left to start Upton's Sandwich Shop on the corner of Church and Main.

Valade's new eatery was initially located in the rear of the terminal, occupying about a third of the total floor space. The restaurant was known as the Central Terminal Restaurant, but most people just called it the Terminal Restaurant. Valade ran it until he entered military service in 1942. Two men named Gurney and Nichols ran the restaurant during his absence. After spending 41 months in the service, Valade returned to running the restaurant in the bus terminal in 1946.

In 1948 Hickok and Boardman, who had occupied the corner of St. Paul and Main next to the terminal for decades, finally relocated to bigger quarters. Valade expanded into their space, and began his long run at that corner, which many today still think of as Valade's corner.

In 1949 Valade gave his restaurant a complete facelift, modernizing it inside and out. His modern corner restaurant featured eleven booths of various sizes along the south wall, an undulating counter with 18 stools, a higher counter with nine stools and a stand up area. Capacity was around 85 in all. A newsstand and candy counter was tucked into the corner by the front entrance. The exterior was finished in a sleek white glass with a marble faced base. Across the top in dark block letters against the white glass were the words "Valade's Terminal Restaurant." The restaurant had an opening into the bus terminal so that the many passengers that came and went daily had easy access to the restaurant without going outside.

In 1957 Valade opened a new restaurant on the other side of the terminal, called Valade's Cafeteria. As the name indicates, it offered cafeteria style ordering, with seating for 130. Like his Terminal Restaurant, which continued to operate on the corner, it was accessible to the terminal via an interior passageway. There was also an entrance on the north side for the Hotel Huntington, whose patrons it was also intended to serve.

Valade's was a very popular breakfast spot for several decades. It was open late, so many would go there after a movie or a few drinks at a bar to get a late night snack. And of course, countless bus travelers enjoyed the cuisine.

In 1971 Valade sold his restaurant to Seward Family Restaurants, a Rutland based chain. Valade's served its final meals on October 17, 1971.

Photo from the James Detore Archive/UVM Silver Special Collections.

The bright, crisp exterior of Valade's Terminal Restaurant after its 1949 facelift.

The Sirloin Saloon

Restauranteur Tony Perry was painstaking in his preparation for the opening of his new restaurant on Route 7 in Shelburne. He designed the exterior of his building in the style of a Western saloon, befitting the name. He grew up near Aspen, Colorado, and had an affinity for all things Western. He spent several months early in 1970 running ads soliciting for stained glass, Tiffany lampshades, Victorian woodwork, and other items to give his interior just the right look. After that he spent several months recruiting and training his waitstaff and kitchen crew. Perry was a veteran in the restaurant business, with two places in Stowe under his belt, and the first Sirloin Saloon, which had opened in 1963 in Manchester. He was meticulous in his approach to the business, making sure that every detail was right. His stated goal was to "serve large portions of the best quality at reasonable prices."

By August of 1970 all was ready, and the Shelburne Road Sirloin Saloon opened for business. It sat 100 diners and 75 in the lounge. As the name indicates, the specialty was beef. The Sirloin purchased its own Western beef, aged it, and had a meat cutter on the premises. The restaurant also featured a self-service salad bar.

The early menu was very limited. One from those days had only nine entrees, seven of which featured beef. Dinner came with the salad bar, warm pumpernickel and French bread, and unlimited coffee. Available "extras" were few, just a baked potato, and two dessert options, rum raisin ice cream or cheesecake.

The restaurant was an immediate hit. It was always packed on Friday and Saturday nights, and since reservations were only available for special occasions like Valentine's Day and Mother's Day, there was often a long wait for a table. But the spacious lounge provided a pleasant place to have a drink and wait, although that was sometimes full as well.

A third Sirloin Saloon was opened in Rutland, and Perry's Fish House followed, which was a little further toward Burlington along Route 7. Perry also opened Sweetwaters, in downtown Burlington. All five of his Vermont restaurants as well as four out of state were overseen by the Perry Restaurant group, which also had their offices on Route 7 in Shelburne.

In 1999 Perry sold his nine restaurants to a group of his former managers who formed a company known as Hospitality Well Done. Their purchase was financed by a loan of $17.3 million from an Idaho based finance company called Amresco Finance. Sweetwaters, Perry's Fish House and a Connecticut steak house remained under the sole ownership of the president of Hospitality Well Done, and were not covered by the terms of the loan.

The debt burden proved to be too much, and in 2002 Hospitality Well Done defaulted. An extended legal battle with Amresco ensued, but in 2005 Hospitality Well Done relinquished seven of its restaurants, including the Shelburne Sirloin Saloon, to Amresco. The restaurant remained open for a few more years, doing good business, if not quite like its glory days. But in 2008 Amresco closed the Sirloin Saloon, ending the 38 year run of one of the favorite dining spots ever in this area. The last meals it served were to two pre-booked bus tours, which had to be honored. Those 100 out-of-towners were the last to savor the food at the Sirloin Saloon.

Another operator opened in the old Sirloin building and ran it for a while as the Shelburne Steakhouse and Saloon. After they closed the building sat vacant for years, slowly sagging and deteriorating. It was finally torn down in November of 2022.

Photograph from rogerkenner.ca.

The Sirloin Saloon in Shelburne, with its family of bears out front and its full parking lot, which was normal for most of its 38-year run.

Howard Johnson's

Howard Johnson's opened their first restaurant in Burlington in 1942. It was located on Shelburne Road, on the corner of what is now Prospect Parkway. The Burlington location was about the 150th restaurant opened by the Massachusetts chain. All of their restaurants from Maine to Florida featured the same colonial architecture, complete with central tower, weather vane and clock. But the thing that made Howard Johnson's stand out was their signature bright orange roof of Spanish tile. Burlington contractors Wright and Morrissey constructed the building using Howard Johnson's plans.

The knotty pine interior exuded warmth and coziness. An article about the opening indicated that when Howard Johnson's first opened, diners could see Lake Champlain through the restaurant's windows. The interior featured a soda fountain counter, as well as tables. It seated around 100, including a dozen stools at the soda fountain counter. Ho Jo's trademark items such as their 28 flavors of ice cream and their fried clams were among the many offerings on their extensive menu. A very large neon sign stood by the side of the road.

Howard Johnson's proved to be very popular, and in 1959 a large new wing was added. Called the family dining room, the additional booths in this space increased capacity to 170. So things were going well for Howard Johnson's on Shelburne Road.

But just three years later, the segment of the new Interstate 89 running through the Burlington area opened to traffic. National chain hotels and restaurants had been following a business model for some time that dictated location of their outlets as close to interstate exits as possible. Burlington was no exception, and the two vacant parcels of land bordering the new cloverleaf intersection were immediately snapped up by Holiday Inn and Howard Johnson's. In 1963 a modern new Howard Johnson's motor lodge opened there. In addition to the motor lodge, there was a restaurant. It featured the signature orange roof, but in a very modern design. A space age style spire topped the roof. Business was so good that the motor lodge expanded less than one year after opening.

Despite the opening of the Interstate, Shelburne Road continued to be a vital artery in and out of Burlington. The old Howard Johnson's was still busy enough for the corporation to keep it going, in addition to the new motor lodge and restaurant by the cloverleaf. In 1976 The Liberty Tavern opened at Shelburne Road, coincident with the nation's bicentennial, and in an apparent move to increase the bar business of the restaurant.

Eventually, as dining trends changed and more and more national fast food chains opened on Shelburne Road, business declined to the point where Howard Johnson's decided to close the Shelburne Road location. The last day in business was November 25, 1984.

The photo is from the James Detore Archives/UVM Silver Special Collections.

The Shelburne Road Howard Johnson's in 1947. The specialties of the house are prominently displayed on their large roadside sign.

The Dog Team Tavern

Even though the Dog Team was not in Chittenden County, I'm including it because there is a Burlington connection to its founding, and just about everyone in Chittenden County ate there at some point in the 75 years it was in operation. So I'm going to take the liberty of telling its interesting origin story.

When most people think of the Dog Team Restaurant, they remember the sticky buns, the relish wheel, or ordering from the chalkboard menu.

But most probably don't know that the story of the Dog Team involved an orphan from Burlington, a Confederate colonel, and a British knight, whose lives intersected and led to the founding of this iconic Vermont restaurant.

Rosamond Hill was born in Burlington in 1857. At an early age she lost both of her parents and went to live with her married sister in Chicago. There she eventually met Col. Edmund McClanahan, a veteran of the Confederate army. After the Civil War he returned home to Tennessee, but everything he had prior to the war had been destroyed. So he migrated north and ended up in Chicago to try to rebuild his life. He met and married the young Rosamond from Burlington, who was 20 years his junior. They had two children, a boy who died at three from tuberculosis, and a daughter Anne.

Wilfred Grenfell was born in England in 1865 and graduated from medical school in 1888. Shortly after, he was assigned to Newfoundland as part of the Royal National Mission to Deep Sea Fishermen. He would devote the rest of his life to helping the inhabitants of northern Newfoundland and Labrador. Anne McClanahan met Dr. Grenfell on a trip to England and they were soon married. Like her mother before her, Anne married a man twenty years older than she was.

Dr. Grenfell spent 40 years (Anne 25) in Labrador and Newfoundland ministering to the native peoples, establishing hospitals, orphanages, nursing stations and other facilities in one of the bleakest regions on earth. Often there were no roads and the only way to get to his patients was by dog team, which is where the name of the restaurant came from. For his work Grenfell was knighted in 1927. He was like a secular saint, in fact he even has a feast day on the Episcopal liturgical calendar.

Eventually his age and health prevented him from returning to Labrador. Sir Wilfred and Lady Grenfell settled into their new life, wintering in Boston and spending the rest of the year on Lake Champlain in Charlotte. The Vermont connection came about as a result of her mother's Burlington roots. Dr. Grenfell still oversaw the network of care facilities that he had established in the far north. Always wanting to do more, they came up with the idea of selling native products with the proceeds going to support their charities in Canada.

This was the idea that led to the first Dog Team Tavern. I say first because the one we all remember was the second Vermont Dog Team. The first one opened in 1931 on Route 7 in Ferrisburgh. An old farmhouse was fixed up and Labrador-made rugs, carvings, blankets and other articles were sold there. You could also of course get a meal. In the early years Lady Grenfell served as hostess when she was in town, and even her mother Rosamond greeted patrons before she passed away. A full sized dog sled sat in front of the tavern, which in a bit of irony was closed in winter. There were also two other Dog Team Taverns in Connecticut with the same mission.

The tavern was very successful. The Grenfells were very well known, maybe the most famous people living in Vermont at that time, and people came from all over to support their venture. Soon plans were underway for a new Dog Team, this time in a brand new building designed and built as a tavern. In addition to an area for the sale of native products, there was a large restaurant and eleven guest rooms. This one, three miles north of Middlebury at Brookside in the Town of New Haven, is the one that people remember. It opened in 1936, and was still a seasonal establishment. Unfortunately Lady Grenfell died two years later at age 53. Sir Wilfred followed in 1940. In 1946 the International Grenfell Association sold the tavern to private owners. They had to wait to install a bar because New Haven was still a dry town in 1946.

As to the restaurant itself, it was famous for many things. As you sat down, a server rolled a relish wheel over to your table. These wheels were actually old "clock reels" that were used for winding yarn. At the end of each "spoke" hung a small bucket with one of six appetizers, usually cottage cheese, pickled beets, red kidney beans, cabbage salad or sauerkraut, and corn relish. There were occasional variations. Next up was a huge, gooey, cinnamon sticky bun that the waitress pulled from a tray

Author's collection.

The interior of the Dog Team, with its signature relish wheel parked next to one of the tables. The day's specials are written on a chalkboard on the wall. Generations of Chittenden County residents made the drive to New Haven to eat at this unique restaurant.

with tongs and plunked in front of each diner. If you ate that, and even some of the relish wheel offerings, you probably were pretty full by the time the entrees came.

The specialty of the Dog Team was prime rib, but no matter what you ordered, the portions were huge. The sides, mashed potatoes and vegetable du jour, were served family style. Dinner also included a salad and small loaves of bread. Doggy bags were a brisque business at the Dog Team.

Diners flocked to the Dog Team from all over, drawn by the quality and quantity of the food, and the uniqueness of the experience. Even if you had no idea of the history, the Dog Team was a place that most people loved just as a restaurant, and returned to again and again.

The Dog Team passed through several sets of owners after the Grenfell years. It was always a seasonal place until the final owner opened it year round in 1987. The restaurant was added to the National Register of Historic Places in 2002. Four years later it was destroyed in a fire. Dozens of priceless artifacts from the Grenfell years were lost in the blaze, as well as the life of the Dog Team's Owner.

The Tower Restaurant

The Tower started in 1967 at the easily remembered address 1234 Williston Road. It featured a barnboard exterior, with the signature "tower" in front that really looked more like a silo than a tower. Their specialty was pizza, along with other Italian dishes and a wide variety of subs and sandwiches. They even served breakfast.

By the early 70s two more branches had been added. One virtually identical to the Williston Road building opened on Pearl Street in Essex Junction next to the shopping center, and the other was in the Ethan Allen shopping center on North Avenue. For a time they also had a branch at the corner of St. Paul and Main Street, where Valade's used to be. Another Tower opened on the Barre-Montpelier Road which also featured the tower in front.

The Tower's 18 year run ended in 1985 when it was sold to Lee Zachary and became Zachary's Pizza.

Author's Collection.

The Tower Restaurant on Williston Road. One of several Tower locations in Chittenden County.

Conrad's/Chez Dufais/Deja Vu

Conrad's started in 1946 as Connie's Barbecue at 183-185 Pearl Street. The prior occupant of the building was the Wager Studio, a longtime Burlington photographer. "Connie" was Conrad LaBelle, who was highly trained in the food business. Connie's served typical American food, burgers, fries, hot dogs and apple pie. One year after opening Connie's was sold to Luther Shattuck, who had been running an IGA market on Catherine Street.

Conrad LaBelle filled the years by selling real estate, running a pet shop, and running for alderman. But in 1958 he re-opened a restaurant at his old Connie's Barbecue location. It was called Conrad's Coffee House, which was a bit misleading, because it was far from just a coffee house. The place featured a snack bar, a pastry shop (LaBelle was a trained baker), a dining room, and a bar with a lounge (the Orchid Lounge). LaBelle's building wasn't that small, but because he packed so many different things into it, each section was very small. The bar only had five stools, for example. In another room a shuffleboard table took up most of the floor space. But Conrad's became a popular spot, and is well remembered by many old enough to have experienced it.

In 1966 LaBelle sold his restaurant to Peter Dufais. He was a Dutch immigrant who had been the manager of the Hotel Vermont. He renamed the Pearl Street restaurant Chez Dufais. He opened up the space and ran part of it as a place for live music and dancing, which he dubbed the Tivoli Lounge. Chez Dufais was noted for its gigantic deli sandwiches, and the wide variety of local musicians who performed at the Tivoli Lounge (later renamed the Living Room). In an echo of the Mill in Winooski, Chez Dufais' ads proclaimed it to be internationally famous.

In 1973 Peter Dufais closed Chez Dufais and left the area. The new owner of the building, Brian Fox, oversaw a remarkable transformation of the building to create his dream restaurant called Déjà Vu.

The former Conrad's/Chez Dufais was a pretty ordinary looking building from the outside. But after Fox was finished, the interior would become extraordinary.

Starting when he was 29, woodworker Fox spent three years crafting the interior from rock maple, brass, and stained and etched glass. He incorporated salvaged architectural elements from old buildings he had helped demolish. When Deja Vu opened in the mid 70s, it set a new standard. Fox was a meticulous craftsman who took no shortcuts. A good example is the hardwood flooring that went into Deja Vu. Instead of using a power nail gun to install it as is normally done, the floorboards were screwed down using a three step process. A hole was drilled for each screw, the screw was then screwed into the hole, and the hole was covered by a wooden plug. This process was repeated 9,000 times to install the floor. Portions of the new restaurant were ripped out and re-done when Fox was not satisfied with the quality.

Even so, he was far from impressed with his own project. He mused about craftsmanship in an interview just before Deja Vu opened. "I've done something that's mediocre for the turn of the century. I've done something that was commonplace not too long ago, and I've fallen short. I think the craftsmanship, for today, is very good. But by the old standards it's average. There are so many old buildings and old things that make me feel so humble." Brian Fox belonged to another era.

Maybe to him it fell short, but to most, Deja Vu was a work of art. Fox estimated it would take ten years of good business to make back what he had put into Deja Vu.

In 1984 he sold Deja Vu to Burlington restauranteur Carl Capra (Carbur's). After Capra's untimely death in 1985 his estate sold Deja Vu to Robert and Pat Fuller, owners of Pauline's on Shelburne Road. Several other restaurants have been in the space since.

Photo from the James Detore Archive/UVM Silver Special Collections.

Conrad's Coffee House on Pearl Street. The building would later be the location of Chez Dufais and Déjà Vu.

What's Your Beef/What Ales You

In the fall of 1971 Francis "Jay" Robinson was in Vermont visiting friends, one of whom was a real estate agent. On a lark they visited a restaurant that was for sale, the old Sugar House location in the basement of the Hotel Vermont. The owners, Jan Rozendaal and Richard Corley had a recent bad experience with the former tenant and were eager to sell. The next day Robinson gave Corley a check for the restaurant, asked him not to cash it for a while, and headed back to Philadelphia, where he was working in a steakhouse.

He contacted 21-year-old Eddie Loeffler, who he'd only known for a few weeks, and asked him if he wanted to come to Vermont to help him run his new restaurant. Four weeks later the pair headed to Vermont, and What's

Your Beef opened in November of 1971. In keeping with the name, the specialty of the house was prime rib.

In the early years Jay and Eddie did everything, cooking, waiting tables, tending bar, even washing the dishes. Eventually they did hire a waitress and a dishwasher. What's Your Beef struggled in those early years, and a strong lunch business was what carried them through that time.

The turning point came in January of 1974 when they ran a $3.99 prime rib special. It was so popular that they kept running it month after month, and their dinner business became firmly established. The rush of new customers revealed another problem: with only a few bar seats, hungry diners were heading elsewhere because there was no place to wait. Their answer was to convert a storage room into a lounge. A separate entrance was cut through the concrete wall, stairs were put in up to the street, and What Ales You was born. It soon became popular in its own right as a destination bar for college students and the post work crowd. Now dinner was booming, they weren't losing diners for lack of bar seating, and the bar they started was a hit in its own right. What's Your Beef was off to the races.

By 1984 they employed 44 people, and that year they served 74,000 pounds of prime rib. In addition to prime rib, the restaurant became known for its iceberg lettuce salad topped with shrimp and chopped egg, their garlic bread, and the thousands of business cards that were tacked up on the old beams that were still there from the old Sugar House days. No one knows how it started, but once a few had been put up, other diners, especially those from out of town, followed suit until the beams, ceiling, and every other available space was virtually covered with cards.

Photo from Vermont Business Magazine/ UVM Silver Special Collections.

What's Your Beef in 1984, the old Sugar House entrance. The tree trunk entrance that used to be to the left has been removed and shingled over by this time.

Jay and Eddie amicably ceased their business partnership in the mid

80s. A few years later each opened a new restaurant on Shelburne Road. Robinson opened What's Your Beef II in the old Victorian Motor Inn mansion, and Loeffler started Jake's Original Bar and Grill in Lakewood Commons.

What's Your Beef's St. Paul Street location closed in 1992 after a memorable 21 year run. Once the mothership was gone, What's Your Beef II dropped the last portion of its name and began referring to itself just as What's Your Beef.

Diners and Sub Shops

Bill's Diner

Bill's Diner in Winooski opened in 1929. It was situated on the south side of East Allen Street, at number 8 East Allen, near the corner of Main Street. The original name was the Twin City Diner, and the original proprietor was Joseph Gabbeitt. He had operated a restaurant on Main Street in Winooski for many years prior. An article about the opening of the diner mentioned that Gabbeitt had obtained one of the trolley cars used by the Burlington Traction Company, which had ceased operations a few months earlier. The old trolley was positioned on Gabbeitt's East Allen Street lot, and outfitted to house his new diner. By the mid 30s, Gabbeitt had changed the name of his diner to Joe's Diner.

By 1939 William "Bill" Gabbeitt had taken over ownership of the diner from his father, and by 1943 the name had been changed to Bill's Diner.

In 1948 Bill Gabbeitt wanted to move on to other ventures, and he sold the diner to Maurice Walsh, who had been in the newspaper business locally for several years. During the preceding nine years Bill's Diner had become a popular Winooski gathering spot, hosting Winooski events such as communion breakfasts and providing minor catering for city events. It was also popular with sports fans and was a ticket outlet for numerous sporting events in the Burlington area. So Walsh kept the name Bill's Diner, a name the diner would retain until it closed decades later.

In April of 1953 Walsh posted a personal ad in the local dailies announcing the "Last Stand of 5¢ Coffee at Bill's Diner."

In 1956 Walsh remodeled and enlarged his diner. He added a new 36-foot long counter, along with seven booths in the new addition, which increased the seating capacity to 80. The exterior look was updated, and Bill's Diner would retain that look for the rest of its time in business.

In 1962 Bill's Diner was substantially damaged in a fire. The damage was covered by insurance, and the diner was renovated and back in business in less than a month.

Bill's was located a short walk from Winoosk's City Hall, and like the Oasis in Burlington, it became a popular gathering place for city politicians to talk politics before and after meetings. By this time the diner was entering its fifth decade in business at the same corner, and had become a cherished Winooski institution.

But in the early 70s Winooski's urban renewal agency notified 15 Winooski businesses that they were located in buildings slated for demolition. Bill's Diner was one of those businesses that would either have to relocate or close. Maurice Walsh elected to close Bill's Diner and open a new (non-diner) restaurant on Shelburne Road.

But Bill's had one last hurrah, as on September 8, 1973, his last day in business, Maurice Walsh rolled back the prices at Bill's Diner to what they had been when it opened in 1929. From the time Bill's opened at 6:00 am that day, the diner was packed as people lined up for 5¢ coffee, and full breakfasts for 45¢. As lunchtime approached, people were ordering beef stew for 25¢, and a hamburger and soda for a quarter. By 4:00 pm they were out of food and the diner closed, marking the end of an era. The following week

Dan Higgins photo.

Somewhere under that modern exterior of Bill's Diner in Winooski was an old Burlington Traction Company trolley car.

the fixtures were auctioned, and a few days later the wreckers tore down Bill's Diner along with all of the neighboring businesses on that block.

Muncy's Diner

The history of Muncy's Diner goes back to the early 1900s when William Anderson and his wife Dora began running a lunch cart in Anderson's home town of Richmond. This was around 1905. In 1911 Anderson rented his Richmond lunch cart to another operator, and moved to Essex Junction, where he opened a new lunch cart to take advantage of the high volume of railroad passengers passing through that busy rail center. The lunch cart was located at 5 Main Street, just east of what is now referred to as the Five Corners.

After operating their lunch cart successfully at the Main Street location for 19 years, in 1930 the Andersons sold it to their daughter Mildred and her husband, Abbott Muncy. They would run the former lunch cart for decades, establishing it as an Essex Junction landmark.

The first order of business was a new name for the eatery, which became Muncy's Diner. The second was to carry on the reputation of the lunch cart

Photorealistic painting by John Baeder.

Muncy's Diner was a popular spot in Essex Junction on Main Street, just steps away from the five corners.

established by the Andersons. The Muncys did more than that as the food they served became well known for its taste and quality, and not just locally. In a 1947 poll of traveling salemen, Muncy's made their list of the top eating spots in the nation.

In 1956, the Muncys expanded the small diner to add more dining space. By this time Muncy's was well established as not just an Essex Junction institution. People were coming from all over Chittenden County for their food, and especially for Mildred's pies. They didn't bother to advertise since there was no need. But other businesses did trade on Muncy's fame in their ads. A barbershop on one side and an insurance firm on the other both included the phrase "next to Muncy's Diner" in their ads.

In 1972 Mildred Muncy died, and that brought an end to the Muncy's 42 year proprietorship of the diner. It did continue on for a few more years under a different owner, but soon Muncy's was out of business. The members of the Andersons and then Muncy families had been serving up their excellent diner fare at that same Essex Junction location for a total of 61 years.

The Oasis Diner

Harry Chafoulous, the second youngest of six sons in a large Greek family, left his homeland for New York City in 1907 at the age of 18. Like many immigrant family names, his was changed due to an immigration officer's impatience. The officer jotted down "Lines" on the immigration paperwork and from that point forward, Harry became Harry Lines.

He quickly made his way to Burlington, where his first business venture was a shoe shine parlor with his brother James, on Church Street right across from City Hall. After five years shining shoes he had accumulated enough money to open a small second floor fruit store above a drug store on the top block.

But in 1916 he and James started doing what they would do for the rest of their working lives, serving food to Burlingtonians. They opened Burlington Lunch near the old Burlington Trust building at Church and College. In 1920 Harry opened the Burlington Sweet Shop on the corner of Church and Main. It was an ice cream parlor and candy shop. The brothers ran both places until 1925 when they closed Burlington Lunch and moved it to 148

James Detore Archive/UVM Silver Special Collections.

Harry Lines poses in front of his new Oasis Diner on Bank Street in 1954.

Church (later the Rusty Scuffer). That same year Harry sold his interest in the Sweet Shop to his brothers and ran Burlington Lunch alone until 1935, when he closed Burlington Lunch and went to work with another of his brothers at the Majestic Diner at 139 Pearl.

After two years he became part owner of the Majestic, but in 1942 he left to run the Miss Burlington Diner on the corner of College and South Winooski (now the Roxy). He ran the Miss Burlington for nearly ten years. In 1950, now 60 years of age, he decided that after 34 years of long hours and standing all day, it was time for relaxation and recreation. He sold Miss Burlington and retired.

But retirement is not for everyone. As he said later, he enjoyed the first few months and then became restless. He took long walks every day, puttered around the house, and took occasional drives. But he finally decided that he needed something to keep him occupied, and that the best way to do that was to go back into business. He purchased a narrow parcel on Bank Street that for decades had been the site of a Chinese laundry. He then ordered a diner from Mountain View Diners in New Jersey to be placed on the site. As the diner neared completion, Harry couldn't wait for it to be ready. "Three years was all I could take", he said of retirement. "In another month I'll be a businessman again." The Oasis opened for business on January 25, 1954.

Once the diner was ready, his son Stratty quit his job at GE to go to work for his father at the new Oasis diner. It would be open from 5 am to 2 am, but Harry admitted that at 63 he would be working fewer hours than he did when he ran Miss Burlington. The Oasis quickly became a favorite spot to get a meal downtown and remained so for its entire 43 year run.

Harry Lines died in 1962. Except for Henry's, he had been involved in every other diner in the city of Burlington. Stratty ran the Oasis until he retired in 1996. He was very interested in politics, and it was easy to get into a friendly debate whenever any political issue came up at the Oasis. So the Oasis became a mandatory stop for just about every politician running for high office at the state or even national level who was visiting Burlington. Presidential candidates such as Bill Clinton and Walter Mondale stopped by to have a bite and talk politics.

The Oasis was sold by the Lines family in 2007. It was briefly the Sadie Katz deli, and at this writing it's El Cortijo, a Mexican restaurant.

Miss Burlington Diner

The Miss Burlington Diner opened on May 24, 1929. The initial proprietor was G.W. Lyons, and the diner was located on the northeast corner of College Street and South Winooski Avenue. Huge illuminated letters on top of the diner, far bigger than those spelling out the diner name, conveyed a simple message: "EAT HERE." By 1935 the diner was one of the rare places in Burlington that was open 24 hours a day.

In 1931 Lyons sold the diner to William Starr, who ran it for 12 years before selling it to Harry Lines. Harry had been involved with the Majestic Diner on Pearl Street prior to Miss Burlington, and would found the Oasis Diner after. In 1950 the Miss Burlington went into receivership, Harry retired from the restaurant business, and his nephew, George Lines, was the next proprietor of Miss Burlington. He bought the diner in partnership with a man named DeBenedette, who ran a tobacco shop in Winooski.

In 1958 the Miss Burlington was sold again, this time to Augustus Turner, a man from Milton. He brought it to Georgia where he set it up

Photo from the James Detore Archive/UVM Silver Special Collections.

The Miss Burlington Diner, on the corner of College Street and South Winooski Avenue.

at the intersection of Route 7 and 104A. He rechristened it as the Miss Georgia Diner. It was there into the 80s, and was known in its later years as the Breaker 19 Diner, an homage to the CB radio craze at the time.

Poncho's

Poncho's Submarine Shop opened at 140 ½ Church Street (right across from City Hall) in 1966. The proprietor was Nelson "Poncho" Camire, a longtime cattle dealer and auctioneer from Barre. Poncho's auction notices were a regular feature in the Free Press for many years.

Author's Collection.

Poncho's Sub Shop at 140 ½ Church Street, right across from City Hall.

Poncho's subs proved to be very popular with the Burlington lunch crowd, as well as with hungry late night bar patrons. Poncho soon opened a second outlet in Mallett's Bay. In this pre-Subway era it was a bit easier for a sub shop like Poncho's to thrive than it would be today.

Poncho Camire retired from the sub business and moved to Florida in 1975. He continued to summer in Vermont and kept his hand in the auction business. But the sub shop on Church Street continued on well after his retirement. Poncho's Subs stayed in business at 140 ½ Church for three different owners after Poncho. The final owner was Dennis Morrisseau, founder of Leunig's. Poncho's finally closed in 1988 and the Red Onion took over the space.

Soda Fountains and Lunch Counters

Soda fountains dispensed soft drinks via lines that mixed carbonated water with flavored syrups, and they also served ice cream treats. They were a staple of drug stores in America for decades. In 1915 there were 17 drug stores in Burlington, and every one had a soda fountain. In addition to all of these drug store soda fountains, there were numerous others.

Soda fountains were a bit difficult to research because most of them did not exist as separate entities. They were located within drug stores, as mentioned, and also as part of large stores, such as Fishman's and Kresge's. These businesses tended to spend their ad dollars on their main business, not the sideline soda fountains within their walls. So there's not much mention of them in the daily papers. There's also a lot of overlap among soda fountains, lunch counters, ice cream bars and such, all of which pumped soft drinks. Lunch counters served sandwiches and hot meals in addition to sodas and ice cream treats. Several restaurants also featured counters that could be considered soda fountains.

So in an effort to sort all of this out, I've included in this section places that were known more for their soda fountains than for serving food, and to be included here, ice cream treats like sundaes and banana splits also had to be served.

Exact numbers are hard to come by, but there were still at least 15 soda fountains within a block of Church Street in the 40s and 50s. So soda fountains lasted well into the time frame covered in this book.

Concord Candy Kitchen

There were many Concord Candy Kitchens, mostly in Vermont, but also in New Hampshire. All of them were either run or owned by members of the very small Greek community of Vermont. The Burlington shop was started by young Greek immigrant Theodore Scutakes around 1900. But there were other, earlier Concord Candy Kitchens started by him in partnership with Peter Stopulos, who immigrated from Greece in 1896 at age 15. The history is a little sketchy that far back, but it is known that the Stopulos/Scutakes partnership opened the first Candy Kitchen in Concord, NH around 1898 (thus the name). Additional stores soon followed in Manchester and Franklin, NH, and in January 1905 they opened one in St. Johnsbury, Vermont. An ad for the grand opening lists Theodore as the proprietor. In September 1905 another Concord Candy Kitchen opened in St. Albans. Unfortunately, Peter Stopulos died suddenly at age 24 in December of 1905. His funeral and burial were in Concord.

Theodore continued the rapid growth of his chain of Candy Kitchens. With Peter gone the focus of the business moved away from New Hampshire and toward Vermont. In early 1906 he signed a lease on the corner of Church and Bank in Burlington to open what would become the main store in the mini chain that he was building. The record is a bit confusing on this. News accounts indicate that the 1906 opening was the first presence of Concord Candy Kitchen in Burlington, but I found a mention of it in Burlington as early as 1902. Other accounts date the Burlington shop to 1900. In any event, by 1906 the Concord Candy Kitchen started business at 80 Church Street, the Burlington location they would occupy for nearly 60 years. There already was a Burlington Candy Kitchen, so he named it the Concord Candy Kitchen like his previous locations. Theodore relocated from Concord to run the Burlington store.

When the Church Street shop opened Theodore promised that his store would have the largest soda fountain in Burlington, and in November he made good on that promise by installing a 20 foot long fountain. Ads indicated that all candy and ice cream were made on the premises (in the basement), although that was not unusual for candy shops of that era.

The Burlington shop became very popular with teenagers, and with Cathedral High School and BHS within easy walking distance, there were plenty of them around.

Theodore Scutakes died in 1942. His son Peter Stokes, who had Anglicized his last name, took over operation of the shop. The store was completely renovated in 1950. By that time candy was no longer made on the premises, and the emphasis was more on the soda fountain/lunch counter. Eventually tastes changed as drive-ins and suburban competitors became more popular. The move of Cathedral High out of downtown in 1959 certainly didn't help. The Concord Candy Kitchen closed on April 1, 1961.

Years later one of Theodore's daughters said in an interview that the Concord Candy Kitchens served as a kind of pipeline to expand the tiny Greek community in Vermont. Theodore's relatives would be brought over to be trained in the Burlington store, then set up as managers of branch locations, which they eventually bought from Theodore. This began even before Peter's death in 1905 when Charles Stopulos came to St. Johnsbury, worked in the Candy Kitchen there and soon opened his own restaurant a few doors down. A branch was opened in Waterbury in 1914 and was run by Vasily Ducas. The Middlebury store, opened in

Photo from the James Detore Archive/UVM Silver Special Collections.

The Concord Candy Kitchen on the corner of Church and Bank Street was a Burlington institution for 60 years. The wall signage was done by Ben Zion Black, longtime Burlington sign painter and the artist who painted Burlington's "lost mural", now at Ohavi Zedek synagogue. Note the large showcase for the Majestic Theatre showing the features playing on their screen just down Bank Street.

1915, was run in partnership by Harry Scutakes and James Foundas. Peter and John Cunavelis came from Greece in 1910 to run the St. Johnsbury store after apprenticing in Burlington. Peter's son John was a well known sportswriter in Burlington. He was born in St. Johnsbury, and worked in the Concord Candy Kitchen there prior to coming to Burlington to attend UVM. The Concord Candy Kitchen in St. Johnsbury lasted nearly as long as the Burlington shop.

Young's Pharmacy

In 1909 E.R. Young, a pharmacist with 13 years' experience in Burlington, opened Young's Pharmacy at 132 Cherry Street. The store was located in the ground floor retail space of the Sherwood Hotel building.

The very next year Young installed a soda fountain in his new pharmacy, undoubtedly to keep up with the competition, as virtually every other drug store in town had a soda fountain. Young's was described as "artistic," made of onyx and mahogany with a marble counter.

Photo from the James Detore Archives/UVM Silver Special Collections.

The soda fountain at Young's Pharmacy on Pearl Street, which was Young's third location, and by far its longest lasting.

In 1917 Young's moved from Cherry Street to 68 Church Street. The space had previously been a sporting goods store, and Young gutted the space and immediately installed his soda fountain to be ready for the opening of his new store. Young's promoted their new location and their soda fountain by advertising their "Special 68, a sundae that will make you glad you're living."

Young's was a bit unusual in that they heavily advertised their soda fountain. Most of the other pharmacies in town promoted their medicines, but barely mentioned their soda fountains.

In 1936 Young's relocated once again, to 184 Pearl Street, their final location. In the ad announcing their grand opening, soda fountain specials were prominently mentioned: 15¢ for a banana split, a jumbo ice cream soda, or a tulip sundae. Tulip sundaes were named for the tulip shaped glass they were served in.

The soda fountain at the Pearl Street pharmacy was modern, using enameled steel panels in several colors and a Formica counter banded in stainless steel in place of the old fashioned marble and mahogany one. The fountain featured ten stools, about average for a drug store fountain, and offered a wide variety of ice cream flavors and toppings. In keeping with their long emphasis on their soda fountain, an exterior photo of Young's from the 40s shows prominent signage indicating "Ice Cream Bar" on the front and side of the building, far more prominent than any signage for drugs or prescriptions.

As the decade of the 60s dawned, soda fountains were rapidly going the way of the horse and buggy. The one at Young's endured until 1966, at which point it was removed and the fixtures sold.

Liggett's Rexall Drug Store

Liggett's tenure in Burlington went back to 1924 when they bought out O'Sullivan's Drug Store, which went back to before 1900. They were located one door north of the corner of Church and Cherry.

In 1937 Liggett's erected a new building next door, replacing an old wood frame building that had stood on that corner for many years. Mrs. Julian Lindsay contracted with Frank L. Austin to design the new structure, which was of steel frame and brick construction. Contractors Wright and

James Detore Archive/UVM Silver Special Collections.

The striking mirror like black glass storefront of Liggett's Rexall drug store in 1948.

Morrissey were able to fulfill a very demanding construction schedule, completing the building in three months. The national chain Liggett's Rexall took out a long term lease on the building.

The most outstanding feature of the new store was the Carrara glass exterior. Pioneered by Abraham's five years earlier, this black glass exterior would be adopted by dozens of downtown Burlington businesses over the years, either using genuine glass, or enameled steel panels that mimicked the look.

In the case of Liggett's it was genuine glass, with black as the dominant color scheme. The lighter colored panels above the windows were orange, which was a trademark color of the Rexall chain. The black glass shimmered with a mirror like finish. The buildings across Cherry Street were reflected in the Liggett's storefront. The glass facade was removed in a 1968 renovation of the building. Years later, when one of Bove's black glass panels was broken, a salvaged panel from Liggett's was used to do the repair.

Like nearly all downtown drug stores back in those days, Liggett's had a soda fountain. Theirs was of moderate size, with 13 upholstered stools, along with a few tables. It featured a marble front and counter.

Liggett's Rexall closed on September 10, 1977 after 40 years of business on this corner. Ask people of a certain age if they remember Liggett's and if they do, it's likely that the first thing they mention will be the soda fountain.

James Detore Archive/UVM Silver Special Collections.

The soda fountain staff at Liggett's line up behind the counter for a photograph in 1948.

The Kelley Pharmacy

The Kelley Pharmacy was located at the corner of Bank and Church. That corner featured a pharmacy going back to 1860. The early proprietors included names such as Lord and Jones, Jones and Riley, and Beaupre and Lowry. Following them, the pharmacy was under the name of R.B. Stearns and then Beebe Drugs. There was a soda fountain as early as 1871 when it was R.B Stearns. The name that remains in living memory though, is the Kelley Pharmacy.

Francis J. Kelley had started working at the pharmacy in 1907 when it was R.B. Stearns. Kelley was 14 years old, and Mason Beebe was the store manager. In 1916 Beebe purchased the store and Kelley became the head pharmacist. The Beebe Pharmacy also featured a soda fountain for its entire existence. Mason Beebe died in 1930 and in 1931 Kelley purchased the store from his estate, but kept the name Beebe.

In 1942 there was a major fire that caused extensive damage to the store. Kelley rebuilt the store with a sleek, modern look. He relocated the entrance, which had been at the corner. The new entrance fronted on Church Street in the middle of the store. The storefront was finished with Carrara glass in a combination of black, green, and light grey. It joined a number of other downtown stores using this material to modernize their appearance. At this point Kelley removed the old soda fountain and installed an entirely new one, carrying on the long tradition of corner drug store soda fountains in Burlington. And at this point the store was renamed The Kelley Pharmacy.

Francis Kelley died in 1955, and in 1958 a man named Scott Brown from Richmond purchased the store, retaining the Kelley name. He ran it for nearly 30 years. In 1959, to devote more floor space to cosmetics, he removed the soda fountain. By this time the era of the soda fountain in America's downtowns was rapidly disappearing into history.

With the removal of the soda fountain, 50% of the Kelley Pharmacy's floor space was devoted to cosmetics, which is probably why my main memory of it is the overpowering smell of perfume as you entered the store.

Photo from the James Detore Archive/UVM Silver Special Collections.

The Kelley Pharmacy is seen right after a 1942 renovation updated the storefront. Another example of the use of Carrara glass to modernize an old, antiquated store.

Fishman's/Centers

I discussed Fishman's in the section on shopping, but their lunch counter merits individual treatment. Installed after Fishman's 1948 renovation and expansion, it sat along the east wall of the store, near the Bank Street entrance. It was one of the longest in Burlington, with over 30 stools. It had every aspect of a soda fountain and much more. Its great length enabled it to feature a wide selection of ice cream and soda varieties. Signage in the huge store pointing the way to it simply referred to it by the word "Fountain," but Fishman's was a true lunch counter as you could get a wide variety of meals there, from burgers, fries and hot dogs, to a wide variety of sandwiches, and even a turkey dinner.

When Fishman's was converted into Centers in 1961, the soda fountain was largely unchanged, but it was given a name: "The Snackery." It was a true lunch counter with an extensive menu of hot and cold foods.

Like several downtown soda fountains, Centers featured balloons that you could pop when ordering a sundae, banana split or other ice cream treat. The lure was that you might pay as little as 1¢ if you selected the right balloon. But most of the time you only ended up with a nickel or dime off the price. But many still remember the anticipation that popping those balloons added to the experience.

This lunch counter/soda fountain was lost when Centers was destroyed in a 1974 fire.

Photo from the James Detore Archive/UVM Silver Special Collections.

The Snackery was the new name given to the Fishman's soda fountain/lunch counter in 1961, one of the many changes that came with the transition of the store into Centers.

Brown's/Gates Pharmacy

Brown's Pharmacy opened in 1936. It was located in the Strong Building, just to the right of the entrance to the Strong Theatre. It featured a small soda fountain, which it referred to as an ice cream bar. In addition to the eight stools at the counter, there were a few tables and booths. Choices were few due to space limitations. Interior photos of Brown's show only Coca Cola as a soft drink option, as well as coffee, and several flavors of Sealtest ice cream. There were no lunch counter type items offered.

In 1945 a man named Gates purchased Brown's Pharmacy, and it became Gates' Pharmacy. The ice cream bar continued until 1952, at which point Gates relocated to Pearl Street. The building's next occupant, the Dutch Treat Shoppe, maintained the soda fountain, though it lasted only briefly. They were followed by Mintzer's Delicatessen at that location, which did not continue with the soda fountain. In 1960 the space was turned over again, with Carr Portrait Studios as the new tenant. They were there until the Strong burned in 1971.

The small soda fountain at Brown's Pharmacy, located at the western end of the Strong building. Brown's was followed by Gates Professional Pharmacy in this location. Photo from the James Detore Archive/UVM Silver Special Collections.

Upton's

There were two versions of Upton's, both at the same location, on the corner of Church and Main. The most recent Upton's was an arcade featuring pinball machines and foosball tables, which also served ice cream. That

Upton's opened in 1976, but this will be about the earlier Upton's, for which the arcade was named.

In 1939 Charles Upton relocated Upton's Sandwich Shoppe from the bus terminal on St. Paul Street to the corner of Church and Main. He completely renovated his new space, installing a small soda fountain (nine stools) and seven booths. In addition, he had the name "Upton's" rendered in stained glass above the entrances on both the Church Street and Main Street sides. The name remained Upton's Sandwich Shoppe right up until 1953 when Charles Upton closed the business.

Upton's was preceded and succeeded by short-lived businesses (Busy Corner Clothing for example), until the second Upton's opened in 1976 for their run of over 15 years. This, plus that stained glass "Upton's" that was there for decades, may explain why several generations thought of this as "Upton's Corner."

Photo from the James Detore Archive/UVM Silver Special Collections.

Santa greets Burlingtonians with Upton's Sandwich Shoppe/Ice Cream Parlor in the background.

Turner's Drug Store

Turner's merits mention because their soda fountain was described as the most ornate ever installed at any Burlington location.

Louis Turner opened his first drug store at the corner of North Street and Elmwood Avenue around 1930. In 1942 he moved into the former Booth's Drug Store at 172 College Street, across from City Hall Park. He had worked there as an assistant for years before opening his own pharmacy at Elmwood and North.

In an ad he posted upon taking over Booth's, Turner listed the inventory of the new store. It included: "1 soda fountain, where people meet for a delicious soda and ice cream, and fellowship."

The soda fountain dated back to 1902, and was said to be one of the oldest still operating in the city. It was made from ornately carved onyx and marble. During the war, Turner was required to keep detailed records for the Office of Price Administration. He reported that in 1945 he served 132,000 customers at his soda fountain.

In 1958 the building housing Turner's was sold to the Chittenden Trust Company, which wanted to demolish the building to create space for their new drive-through bank outlets. The neighboring Merchants Bank would also have drive-throughs in this area, and one for the Burlington Savings Bank would be located at the other end of this cut-through to St. Paul Street.

So Turner's Drug Store, which by now had been renamed the Park Drug Store, closed. The closing marked the end of 152 years of a pharmacy having been located at this address.

Right before the store closed, Turner advertised the sections of his soda

Photo from the James Detore Archive/UVM Silver Special Collections.

Turner's Drug Store next to Abraham's, another longtime Burlington drug store.

fountain for sale. From the ad it appears that it was about 24 feet long. He knew that the time of the downtown soda fountain was passing away, replaced by the drive-in snack bars, so he mentioned in his ad that the marble pieces would make great flagstone if broken up. I have no idea if anyone took him up on his offer.

Kresge's

Kresge's had a big lunch counter that also had every feature of a soda fountain. From the opening of Kresge's in 1933, the store had a large lunch counter that took up the entire north wall of the store. In 1937 the lunch counter was expanded, making it 63 feet long, said to be the largest in the state of Vermont. Thirteen stools were added, bringing the total to 31. The revolving stools had backs, a very unusual feature, and were upholstered in red leather. They lined up against a marble faced counter. Four large fans above the lunch counter cooled the diners during summer, as Kresge's was not air conditioned at this point.

In 1938 the entire interior of Kresge's was destroyed in a huge fire. The firm quickly rebuilt their store, enlarging it to a depth of 100 feet. Again,

L.L. McAllister photo archive/UVM Silver Special Collections

The last soda fountain/lunch counter at the S.S. Kresge store on Church Street. At 68 feet, it was the longest one in the state.

along the north wall of the store they installed a lunch counter that was the longest in the state. At 68 feet long, it featured 36 stools, and looked very similar in design to the one lost in the fire. The counter was again of marble, green on the top and pink on the bottom. Meals were prepared in a basement kitchen, and two dumb waiters lifted them up to the lunch counter on the ground floor.

Like at Woolworth's and Fishman's, a wide variety of hot meals, cold sandwiches, ice cream and soda treats as well as pies were on the menu. Kresge's also had the balloon promotion described in the Fishman's section.

In 1964 the Burlington Kresge became Jupiter, a discount division of Kresge's. The Burlington Jupiter closed in 1972. A few years later the Kresge building was torn down to give the Burlington Square Mall an entrance on Church Street.

Sherlock's Pharmacy

Sherlock's was a last minute addition to this book because while going through photos after completing the text, I noticed that a photo of Sherlock's showed a soda fountain. Sherlock's was one of the original stores in the Ethan Allen Shopping Center when it opened in 1954, and it was a great surprise to see that it had a soda fountain.

So there can be little doubt that the soda fountain at Sherlock's Pharmacy was the last one ever to open in Chittenden County, drug store or otherwise. Sherlock's soda fountain featured ten stools and offered a simple menu of sodas, sundaes and sandwiches. Proprietor Merrill Sherlock had no way of knowing of course, that the era of the drug store soda fountain would soon start drawing to an end, and that his new soda fountain was pretty much an anachronism even before it pumped its first soda.

Merrill Sherlock ran his pharmacy until 1963, when he left the area. His drug store then became Plouffe's Pharmacy. It's not known what happened to the 1954 soda fountain, but there's no mention of it in the many ads for Plouffe's that ran over the years.

Photo courtesy of Janie Merola McKenzie/Louie Merola Collection.

Merrill Sherlock poses in his new pharmacy at the Ethan Allen Shopping Center in 1954. It included a ten stool soda fountain. He couldn't have known that the era of the soda fountain would soon be ending.

Bars

Chittenden County has long been the home of several colleges. The University of Vermont and Champlain College call Burlington home. St. Michael's is in Winooski Park, between Winooski and Colchester. For many years, a fourth college, Trinity, added to the student population until it closed in 2001. The presence of these schools meant that the area has been home to thousands of young people for the better part of each year. One of the favorite activities among college students is drinking, so many bars have come and gone over the years to give students options for the many nights they would spend bar hopping during their college years. This section will cover some of the more memorable bars in Chittenden County over the years.

The Hotel Breton

The Hotel Breton was located in a brick federal style building that dated back to the early 1800s. It was known for years as the concert hall, as it was one of the few performance venues in early Burlington. The building was on the Church Street block between College and Bank. It sat way back from Church Street, and was so completely surrounded by other structures that were built up around it over the years that it was nearly invisible. It was accessed via an alleyway that connected it with Church Street. Above the entrance a large neon sign proclaimed the presence of the hotel, and a canopy stretched over the sidewalk from the alley entrance to the curb. The Breton was one of a very few Burlington businesses to ever feature such a canopy.

Known as the Travelers Inn for years, in 1940 Marie Ange Roulliard of Winooski leased the hotel. She renamed it the Hotel Breton, and in 1944 she purchased it. By the mid 50s she had added to the existing bar and grill, opening the Champlain Lounge, a cocktail lounge for dining and dancing, as well as the College Room, whose target audience was obvious. The lounge was on the lobby level, while the College Room was in the basement below. The Breton became a popular spot for UVM students as well as those from other schools.

Eventually the college crowd began to favor the many other bar options that had sprung up over the years, and the Breton fell out of favor. It descended into seediness, and as one article put it, they had trouble with the city, the police, the liquor control boards and the tax collector. The Breton building had been unoccupied for about a year when it burned in December of 1970. It was demolished soon after.

Photo from the James Detore Archives/UVM Silver Special Collections.

The alley leading from Church Street to the Hotel Breton.

The Mill

The Mill Café was started in 1936 by Anthony Wasilkowski. He was a Polish immigrant who had come to Winooski to work at the American Woolen Mills. By 1936 he was able to purchase the large brick building on West Canal Street between Weaver and Mayo Streets. The building dated back to around 1840, and had been built as housing for women workers at the mills. In 1932 the American Woolen Mill Company had auctioned off many properties that they owned near the mills, including this one. Wasilkowski bought the building from the person who had obtained it in that 1932 auction.

There were two stores on the Weaver Street side of the building, a grocery store and a meat market. Wasilkowski knocked out the wall separating the two stores, creating one large space, and there he opened his Mill Café. The name paid homage to the building's role in the long history of the mills in Winooski.

Wasilkowski ran the Mill Café until 1947. At that point Phil and Julie Melanson took over running The Mill. Under the Melansons The Mill survived the closure of the Winooski mills in 1954, and became a favorite hangout for students from UVM, St. Mike's and Trinity, as well as locals. Back in those days the colleges were bursting at the seams from all of the returning GIs, and there still weren't a lot of bar options in the area.

The Mill was also a favorite of New York Giants players in the years that they trained at St. Michael's. Giant owner Tim Mara was a devout Catholic, and had selected St. Michael's for that reason. He hoped that constant contact with the priests on campus would rub off on his players, and also counted on the lack of temptation near the campus to keep his boys on the straight and narrow. But after enduring punishing practices and the spartan dorm at St. Mike's, Giants players regularly made their way to the nearest bar they could find, The Mill.

I'll relate a brief anecdote from the Giants days that was told to me by an acquaintance who has since passed away. The person relating this story was at UVM during the Giants years. He was 6'4', a UVM athlete, and handsome even into his 70s when he related this story. He and a friend ventured over to the Mill to try to "date up" some girls, as they said in those days. They were making excellent progress with two young ladies at their table when all of a sudden there was a tremendous commotion at the front door, where a crowd quickly gathered. One of the girls' friends yelled from the door, "It's Frank Gifford and Pat Summerall." They were two of the Giants young stars and probably two of the most handsome men ever to play in the NFL. The two girls dashed away from the table, leaving my friend and his pal alone with their beers, their plans in tatters.

The Mill featured a huge central fireplace which had a roaring fire going during the colder weather. I always wondered why it hadn't burned down years ago. The sign to the left of the front door read "The Mill Restaurant, Internationally Known." Perhaps a tongue in cheek take on the place's proximity to Canada, but whatever the meaning it seemed to poke fun at the Mill's purported fame. In the Mill's early years patrons started a custom of signing paper plates and attaching them to the walls and ceiling until they were covered.

In 1965 the Wasilkowski family finally sold the Mill building to the Melansons. They retired in 1982 and the Mill was closed after they had run it for 35 years. The new owners renovated the interior using the magnificent woodwork from the Catholic Bishop's house on Williams Street, which had recently been demolished. The first venture, The Mill Cafe and Boarding House, didn't last long, but the next one, The Peking Duck House, had a long run at the former Mill location.

photo by Rebecca Hostettler/National Archives.

The Mill Restaurant, former worker housing on the corner of West Canal and Weaver Streets. 1978

The Chickenbone Café

The Chickenbone was located in an historic building at the corner of King and South Champlain. The building dated to 1815, and had been owned by several significant figures in Burlington's early history, including Timothy Follett, Gideon King, John Pomeroy and Thaddeus Tuttle. From the 1930s through the 50s it housed Glasston's Market, and after that, reportedly a bar called Skinny's, and later, bars called 43 King Street and the A.C. Café. In 1976 it was purchased by David Abdoo, who opened it up as the Chickenbone Café, beginning its memorable run in Burlington.

As to the bar itself, you never heard it called the Chickenbone Café, and rarely the Chickenbone. People just called it "the Bone." A sign on the building featuring a cartoon rooster sporting shades, a cigarette, and a mug of beer spoke to the "bad to the bone" vibe that many associated with it. It was located in what was considered a rough part of town at the time, but the Bone attracted a wide variety of customers, from lawyers and other movers and shakers, to college students, and of course locals. The Bone had many regulars, and Abdoo took care of them via things like the Bone card that allowed them to move to the head of the lines that formed on weekend nights.

The Bone was not without controversy. For years it was a regular source of complaints from neighbors about noise and other disturbances. I can personally attest to this because my father was the alderman for the ward where the Chickenbone was located. When the phone would ring on Friday and Saturday nights it was often someone calling him to complain about the Bone, or its neighbor across the street, The Sheik.

In 1992 David Abdoo lost control of the Chickenbone for a time. Others stepped in to keep the Bone running, but without Abdoo it just wasn't the same. He provided that indefinable quality that made it what it was, a place well remembered by all of its loyal patrons. As of this writing I've been running a Burlington history Facebook group for nearly five years, and every time I post a photo of the Chickenbone, it never fails to generate huge volumes of enthusiastic comments, probably more than just about any other subject. People love to reminisce about their days walkin' on the wild side at the Bone.

When Abdoo sold the Chickenbone in 2000, the buyer, a local non-profit, intended to demolish the building and replace it with affordable housing. The iconic black rooster on top of the Chickenbone was to be auctioned. But a compromise was reached, and only the addition south of the main building was demolished. A single family home was built there by Habitat for Humanity. The portion running up King Street was preserved as an historic site.

Photo from Vermont Business Digest Magazine/ UVM Silver Special Collections

A Chickenbone patron "rides" the gigantic black rooster that sat atop the Chickenbone Café. The 200 pound bird came from California. After the Bone closed it was sold at a charity auction for $7,000. Right after it was sold, it was stolen, but was quickly recovered.

Hannibul's/B.T. McGuire's

Although Hannibul's was only in business for eight years, it's one of the more memorable Burlington bars. The bar opened at 154 Church Street, right across from City Hall, in 1971. Two young guys from Massachusetts, Bill Hunter and Thomas Kennelly, had met at St. Michael's College, where they were both in the class of 1969. In 1971 they started Hannibul's, which was named after Hunter's dog, not the Carthaginian general who tormented Rome. The name of Hunter's hound was spelled slightly differently than that of the ancient general.

Hunter and Kennelly wanted to have a place that would appeal to all, not just to college kids. Obnoxious customers were quickly dealt with, creating a welcoming atmosphere for all. The décor evoked a frontier saloon, but without the rowdiness, and Hannibul's soon developed a loyal following. It had good bar food and became the neighborhood bar for many.

The bar sponsored numerous local sports teams, starting by sponsoring a raft in the Great Winooski River Raft Race of 1971. They followed up by sponsoring softball and basketball teams over their years in Burlington. All of this deepened the bond they were building with locals.

The opening of Hannibul's coincided with the drinking age dropping to 18 in Vermont. So they, like all Burlington bars, prospered from the huge increase in potential customers among the thousands of college students in the area. Hannibul's was routinely packed with customers on the weekends, and long lines to get in were the norm. But Hannibul's was able to avoid becoming just a bar for college drinkers.

The success of Hannibul's resulted in many others trying to emulate their success, and as a result, the cost of opening a bar in Burlington soared. The building housing Hannibul's sold for $35,000 in 1970, the year before Hannibul's opened. Six years later the building sold for $200,000, and the estimated value of the building plus the businesses in it was $400,000. Hunter and Kennelly had opened Hannibul's on a mere $6,000.

In December of 1979 Hannibul's served its last drinks. Hunter opened a restaurant in Nantucket called the Atlantic Café, and after Hannibul's closed, he literally took the name with him. He moved the Hannibul's sign down to Nantucket, where it hung in his new bar. It was replaced at 154 Church by the Mexican themed Peceras.

Hannibul's left a lot of great memories in Burlington, and if you took

Author's collection.

The entrances to Hannibul's (downstairs), and B.T. McGuire's (upstairs), two of Burlington's most popular 70s bars, were located right across from City Hall.

a poll to name the best bar ever in Burlington, it's likely that it would get more than a few votes.

Hunter and Kennelly followed up the success of Hannibul's by opening B.T. McGuires in 1972. It was located upstairs from Hannibul's at 152 Church Street. Its only presence on the ground level was a door leading up the stairs to the bar, kind of Burlington's version of "Upstairs, Downstairs." A wide assortment of establishments had occupied the upper and lower floors in the 1878 building that housed Hannibul's and McGuire's. The most recent notable pair was the Oyster Bar downstairs, and the Pearl Room upstairs.

McGuire's was opened by the pair to be more of a restaurant than bar. The food offerings were to be much wider that what was offered at Hannibul's, served up in a more refined atmosphere. One veteran observer described McGuire's as one of Burlington's original quiche and salad eateries. So whether you consider B.T. McGuire's a bar or a restaurant depends on your perspective, or perhaps when you experienced it.

By 1978 Hunter and Kennelly had sold B.T. McGuire's to Michael Cain and a partner. By then they were concentrating on their biggest lift so far, the renovation of a large 1880s building on Battery and King into what would become the Ice House Restaurant. Cain was Grand Isle

State's Attorney at the time. He ran McGuire's until 1986, when he and another partner sold McGuire's and Peceras to Faraj Nakhleh. Nakhleh transformed it into the Cordoba-B.T. McGuire's Tequila Bar, which was gone not long after it opened, marking the end of the B.T. McGuire name. An Irish themed bar called Oh! Malley's moved into the McGuire space, but was gone by the end of 1988.

The Red Dog

In 1964 Jack DuBrul bought an old livery stable building at 163-165 Church Street. The old structure on lower Church had housed a bowling alley upstairs for years, and a garage on the ground floor. DuBrul was an avid race car driver, and he opened his Speed and Race Engineering shop in the former garage space. In 1965 Jack's brother David opened a night club upstairs in the old bowling alley space, which he named the Red Dog.

The Red Dog offered live entertainment nightly, and the club quickly became a favorite stop in the Burlington bar scene. The ever changing bands from around the region were a big hit with locals and college students. Unfortunately, the club became a frequent target of noise complaints from the landlord and tenants of a building just to the north. Complaints about noise would dog DuBrul off and on for the entire time that the Red Dog was in operation. He tried everything he could do to alleviate this issue, including installing sound deadening and monitoring equipment, but the complaints continued,

Author's Collection.

The Red Dog, located upstairs in a former bowling alley, was a popular spot largely due to its ever changing live entertainment featuring bands from around the region and beyond.

eventually causing the Red Dog to lose its entertainment license for ten days. It was a nearly impossible situation for Dubrul due to the lack of a very specific noise ordinance for the city. As long as the neighbors complained, he was always in danger of losing his entertainment and/or liquor license.

Finally, in 1975, no doubt fed up with it all, DuBrul sold the very popular night club and moved on. The time of the Red Dog was over after ten years, although other clubs moved into the space in later years.

The Movies

Up until the 50s, if you wanted to see a movie, you had to go to Burlington or Winooski. Burlington's downtown area had many small movie theaters during the silent movie era. There were at least ten theaters that came and went between 1905 and 1920, all but one either on Church Street, or within a block of it. As the talkies took over the movies, Burlington saw the establishment of four substantial movie theaters, the Majestic, the Strong, the State, and the Flynn. Another existed right across the river in Winooski, the Strand. All of these are gone except for the Flynn, which hasn't been a movie theater for many years.

But the 50s and the car culture brought a new phenomenon to the area, the drive-in movie. The first drive-in theater in Chittenden County was the Sunset Drive-In in Colchester, which opened in the spring of 1949. It's still in business, so we'll concentrate on the three other drive-ins that are no longer around.

So this section will begin with telling the stories of the traditional downtown theaters that are gone. Then we'll move into the arrival of the drive-ins, and after that we'll delve into the transition of movie theaters from Burlington to the suburbs.

The Strand

Winooski had its own theater from the very early days of the silent movie era. In 1908 the Comique opened at 66 Main Street. Later, this site was the location of the Grand Union in Winooski for many years. After a few months the Comique became the Nickel Theatre, then by 1918 it was the New Nickel, and in 1919 it became the Strand.

Once the theater became the Strand, it would soon become almost exclusively a movie house, although it occasionally still hosted live shows. In 1932 the seating capacity was increased from 80 to 380, still much smaller than even the smallest theater in Burlington, the State. But that new capacity was about normal for other Vermont cities the size of Winooski.

With the coming of the talkies, the Strand was able to hold its own competing with its much larger competitors in the Queen City. It was regularly able to screen first run movies featuring well known Hollywood names that would be able to entice people to head to Winooski for a show at the Strand. But by the 50s the Strand seemed to be in decline. Throughout the 40s, ads for Strand features appeared alongside those of the large Burlington venues. All five theaters featured large illustrated ads for their films. By the 50s, the Strand ads had been reduced to tiny, text only ads set off at the right hand margin of the movie page.

Then on Saturday, March 24, 1956, the end came for the Strand as it was destroyed in a fire. There was talk of rebuilding, but that fire marked the end of movie theaters in Winooski.

Image courtesy of the Theatre Historical Society of America.

The Strand Theatre in Winooski in 1941. It was able to compete with the four movie houses in Burlington for most of its long life on Main Street.

The Majestic Theatre

The Majestic Theatre stood on Bank Street, between Center Street and South Winooski Avenue. Much smaller than the Strong, which was just down the street from it, the Majestic's initial seating capacity was only 600. Although it did have a stage for live shows, from the day it opened, May 16, 1912, the Majestic was primarily a movie house. It featured a six piece orchestra that accompanied the silent movies featured in its early years.

It was built by J.R. Lockwood, a Burlington carriage maker, and E.R. Hutchinson, who had made a success of operating the Bijou Theatre out of a business block on College Street.

The much larger and ornate Strong was still primarily featuring live shows, so the Majestic was able to carve a niche for itself as a movie house. A year after opening, Lockwood and Hutchinson removed the stage and repositioned the movie screen onto the back wall, expanding capacity to over 700.

In 1916 they acquired an additional 40 feet of adjoining land running down South Winooski Avenue. Onto this new parcel the Majestic was expanded again, adding a new stage with opera boxes on either side, along with additional floor seating. The work was done during winter and the theater remained opened throughout, not losing a single day of business.

Photo from the James Detore Archive/UVM Silver Special Collections.

The interior of the Majestic Theatre in Burlington in 1940.

The addition increased capacity to nearly 1,000. The relatively small Majestic building managed this large capacity mainly by having a tiny lobby.

In 1919 the Majestic was sold for $100,000 to the Queen City Realty Corp. This was a consortium of a dozen Burlington businessmen, headed by John J. Flynn. Other investors included Elias Lyman, Warren Austin, Thomas Unsworth, and J.S. Patrick.

In 1925 Wurlitzer's largest two keyboard organ model was installed at the Majestic, replacing the orchestra for silent movie accompaniment.

The Majestic can claim two distinctions in Burlington cinema history. It was the first theater built as a stand-alone movie house, and it was also the first Burlington theater to install the equipment needed to screen "talkies." Except for a one time demonstration described in the Strong Theatre section, the Majestic was where the first talkie in Burlington was featured, 1929's "The Wolf of Wall Street."

The Majestic prospered under the new ownership for several years. But by the late 20's that prosperity highlighted the limitations of the Majestic. Its talking pictures were so popular that several times a week the theatre could not accommodate the numbers of people trying to attend a showing. The huge Strong Theatre down the street still had not installed sound equipment, leaving the huge and growing market to the Majestic and the much smaller and cruder Orpheum.

The owners of Queen City Realty decided to build a second theater in downtown Burlington. The result was the Flynn Theatre on Main Street. When it opened in 1930, it was the first theater in New England specifically designed for movies with sound. It was much larger and more ornate than the Majestic. When the Flynn opened, Queen City Realty's Majestic was immediately relegated to second tier status. That situation was greatly compounded when the Strong pivoted to sound movies and de-emphasized live shows around the same time.

1930 also saw the opening of the new State Theatre on Bank Street. The State was a revitalized reincarnation of the Orpheum, which had been screening films at the Bank Street location since 1917.

So the Majestic was facing three rival theaters, all within a stone's throw of it, and each more attractive than the aging Majestic. The result was that the Majestic started to lose out with audiences. The newer, bigger theaters could outbid the Majestic for the top films, and so for many years it was relegated to showing B movies.

The owners gave the theater a facelift in 1932, but the renovation didn't help much as B movies remained the Majestic's stock in trade. A marquee was added in 1940. The Majestic was the last Burlington theater to get one.

The theater continued as a B movie house for the remainder of its life. But there was a market for B movies as well, and it enabled the Majestic to hang on until 1954. By that point the pioneering Majestic was a distant fourth among Burlington's four theaters. The doors were closed for good after the last showing of the film *Martin Luther* on Friday, November 5, 1954.

After it closed the Majestic sat vacant for over a year with a "for rent" sign on the marquee. There were no takers, and the building was demolished in February of 1956. Cliff Amour's Tire and Battery replaced the venerable movie house. A gas station/convenience store and parking lot still occupy the large footprint of the former theater.

The State Theatre

The 1930 State Theatre would never be confused with a movie palace. It was the smallest theater in Burlington, seating only 600. It didn't have a large, ornate lobby, just a small area between the ticket booth and the theater doors where the concession stand was located.

The ancestry of the State went back to the early days of cinema in Burlington. The theater's roots date back to the 1911 World in Motion Theater located in the New Sherwood Hotel. In 1917 the proprietors of the World in Motion, Mr. and Mrs. Meader Martin, bought the old Walker Block on Bank Street, which had previously been the Burlington Grocery building, from Alfred Perrotta. Perrotta had started the Orpheum Theater in his building just a few months earlier. The Martins ran the Orpheum until 1930, when they renovated it and renamed it the State Theatre.

The State was renovated again in 1939 due to a fire in the block that gutted the Black Cat Café next door. The damage to the State was largely water damage. This renovation removed any decorative touches that remained from the old Orpheum as sound deadening panels were installed on the walls and ceiling, giving the interior a rather plain look. The theater's marquee was also installed as part of this renovation.

Meader Martin died in 1937, but his wife Catherine continued to operate the State until 1951. At this point Ernest Handy started renting the theater while Mrs. Martin retained ownership of the building, which also included the Black Cat Café next door.

When Catherine Martin died, she left the Walker building and the theater to the Roman Catholic Diocese of Burlington. The diocese quickly sold it to Ernest Handy, who had been renting the State for seven years by this point. He would run it until it reached the end of the line.

Despite its small size relative to the rival Flynn and Strong theaters, the State was always able to hold its own in attracting top movies to its screen. A good example of this is the fact that the Vermont premiere of the film version of *The Sound of Music* was held there. This wildly popular movie, with strong Vermont connections was no doubt highly sought after, but somehow the State managed to get it. Maria von Trapp herself attended the opening. The State also hosted the Vermont premieres of *2001: A Space Odyssey* and *The Graduate.*

But toward the end, the State, like other downtown theaters, was struggling in the face of competition from new suburban cinemas. By the mid 70s the theater was reduced to featuring X-rated fare in an attempt to attract customers. The end for the State came on May 1, 1977 when an explosion in the building started a fire that was soon out of control. The entire Walker Block building, including the State and the neighboring Black Cat Café, was destroyed. The fire left Burlington with only one remaining movie theater, the Flynn.

Image courtesy of the Theatre Historical Society of America.

Burlington's State Theatre in 1941. You entered through the triple doors under the marquee and exited through the double doors at the right. The placement of the State's "blade" sign is very unusual. These were normally centered over the marquee, but the State's management centered it on the theater itself, placing it to the right of the marquee.

The Strong Theatre

The Strong has probably the most interesting history of all of Burlington's old theaters. It was lost to fire, but if it hadn't been for an earlier fire it might not have been built in the first place.

In the late 1800s a group of Burlington businessmen built a large roller skating rink on the current site of the Fletcher Free Library. It was built to take advantage of a roller skating craze that had been sweeping the nation for several years. But not long after the Burlington rink was completed the craze faded and the rink became a white elephant. After serving as a furniture warehouse for several years, it became the armory for the local National Guard unit. But then the old rink had to be demolished or moved to make way for the new Fletcher Free Library.

Two brothers, J.J. and J.T. Whalen, bought the building with the intention of moving it. The 72 x 200 foot wooden building was cut in half and moved by horse teams one block down South Winooski Avenue to the corner with Main Street. There the building was placed on a foundation the brothers had built. The old armory was remodeled into an immense auditorium and dance hall, the largest in the state. But just as it was about to open, it was destroyed in a 1902 fire.

When they had considered their next move, the Whalens decided to go big. There was an increasing demand for a ground floor theater in the city. The 1879 Howard Opera House was the city's only high quality performance venue, and its third floor auditorium was seen more and more as a problem in the event of the need to evacuate in case of fire. The brothers engaged Frank L. Austin, a Burlington architect to design a theater to rival or even surpass the Howard. He traveled to theaters all over New England, determined to incorporate the best ideas he saw into his new Burlington theater.

One of the challenges was the site, which was located in the deepest part of a ravine that snaked through the length of old Burlington. Rather than try to fill it in and risk building the new theater on filled land, Austin decided to build a foundation that stepped down the steep embankment into the ravine. This would prove to be a wise decision, as in later years some buildings built on filled ravine land, including the Fletcher Free Library, would face problems due to settling.

The new Strong Theatre was huge, it sat 1500 people, and featured private boxes and two balconies, the only Burlington theater ever to be able to make that claim. The 58 foot wide stage was capable of accommodating even the largest traveling companies. It was the most ornate theater ever built in Burlington, with molded plaster ornamentation on the ceiling, proscenium arch, balcony fronts, opera boxes and throughout the building. Painted scenes adorned the ceiling and proscenium. The stage was lighted by 500 electric lamps. A bridge was constructed over the ravine between the theater and South Winooski Avenue, allowing crews for traveling shows to easily bring their sets and costumes into the backstage area of the theater. A large complex of dressing rooms was located on the back of the building.

A long, wide passage led from the ticket booth in the front to a large lobby just before the auditorium, similar to the way the Flynn is designed.

The theater was the latest word in safety too. It featured 13 lighted exits, and even with a capacity crowd, the entire building could be evacuated in three minutes.

So when the Strong opened in 1904 it was widely praised on all counts. The city had never seen anything like it. The Strong joined the Cahn and

Image courtesy of the Theatre Historical Society of America.

Burlington's Strong Theatre in 1968. Strong Hardware occupied the entire ground floor space to the left of the marquee. The three tenants to the right were John Merola's Barber Shop, Serendipity Gifts, and Carr Portrait Studios.

Grant theater chain, by far the biggest in New England, ensuring that the top acts touring the region would appear there.

Due to all the factors discussed above, the Strong supplanted the Howard Opera House as the city's top performance venue, and the Howard ceased to operate as a performance house the same year the Strong opened.

As movies replaced live shows as the main entertainment in America, the Strong evolved from a Vaudeville house to a movie house. An important event occurred on October 22, 1925, when the first talking movie shown in Burlington was projected at the Strong using the DeForest Phonofilm system. But that was a one-time demonstration event, and the Strong was surprisingly slow to adapt to talkies. Interestingly, Burlington was only the third city in Vermont to get talking movies. Rutland was the first, then Barre. When talkies finally did get to Burlington, it was the Majestic that premiered them. Even the Orpheum (soon to become the State), and the Strand in Winooski had talking pictures before the Strong did. The Strong was the last Burlington theater to install a permanent talking movie system when it finally did so in January of 1930.

A renovation in the 30s muted a lot of the original ornamentation of the interior. A new lighted Art Deco marquee was installed, which extended well out over the Main Street entrance and highlighted the latest features amid an array of flashing lights. A large neon "blade" style sign was installed. Projecting from the front of the building, it ran down from the roof to the top of the marquee, with just the word "Strong" on it. Like the marquee, it was also Art Deco.

The Strong was renovated two more times, once in 1947 after a fire, and again in 1949 in an extensive makeover, which seems to coincide with the closing of the second balcony.

But as the car culture took hold, over time movie patrons came to prefer new cinemas in suburban locations with their acres of free parking. They didn't seem to mind the much smaller screens and basic interiors of the suburban cinemas compared to the old Burlington movie houses. The Burlington movie palaces, the Strong and the Flynn, one block away on Main Street, fell on hard times. The top balcony of the Strong was closed off, condemned as being unsafe. Both theaters became run down and struggled to attract an audience.

But the Strong was a movie house to the end, which came on Saturday, October 9, 1971. "Klute" starring Jane Fonda was on the marquee when an early morning fire completely destroyed the 67 year old landmark. The fire was determined to be arson, one of many such fires that plagued the city in the 70s, claiming the Strong and other historic buildings.

The fire left a literal gaping hole in the city's downtown as the ravine location of the former Strong sat vacant for 15 years. It was finally filled in 1987 when a new office building, Courthouse Plaza, was built on the old theater's site.

Malletts Bay Drive-In

The Malletts Bay Drive-In opened on Bay Road in Malletts Bay in 1949, a couple of months after the Sunset. To entice customers from its Colchester rival, the Malletts Bay "open air auto theatre" boasted about their screen:

Vermont's Largest Outdoor
Motion Picture Screen!
Steel Towers—Custom Made—Tilted

Photo courtesy of Alfred Holden.

The marquee of the Malletts Bay Drive-In shows two of the hundreds of X-rated movies screened there during the 22 years that it featured such films.

On opening night, June 24, 1949, size was again emphasized as the proprietors Eddie Perrotta, Gordon Jarvis and Ozzie Barr proclaimed that they had "Vermont's Largest Auto Theatre", with a gigantic screen. They opened with a double feature, *The Green Grass of Wyoming*, and *The Tender Years*.

I discuss more about the Malletts Bay at the end of this section.

The Mountain View Drive-In

The Mountain View was established by Frank Bernardini and his son Orero. They had been in the restaurant business in the area for years, and Bernardini's was a well established eatery on Pearl Street in Burlington.

In June of 1952 workers graded a large parcel of land on the east side of Routes 2 and 7, about a half mile north of downtown Winooski in Colchester. By the end of July this new "outdoor theater" was ready to open for business. It accommodated 650 cars. This was the fourth drive-in in the

The huge parking area of the Mountain View Drive-in, with Camel's Hump in the distance, illustrating how the place got its name. Photo from the James Detore Archive/UVM Silver Special Collections.

area. It had a gorgeous view of the Green Mountains to the west, which is where the name came from. But movie viewers would be looking in the other direction, and of course they would be attending shows after dark, so the view was a moot point for most.

The first film shown at the Mountain View was a forgotten movie called *The Sniper*, along with an Abbott and Costello short and a cartoon. Drive-ins were the new thing and business was good. The Bernardini family staffed and managed the drive-in. Frank had died in 1963, and son Orero was managing the drive-in. But in 1970 he sold it to SBC Managment Corp. out of Boston. Merrill Jarvis, a local veteran of the theater business, took over as manager.

The Burlington Drive-In

Mr. and Mrs. Ulderic Barrett had been operating the Milton Drive-in on Route 7 in Milton since 1949. In 1956 they decided to relocate to Shelburne Road. So the screen of the Milton Drive-In was disassembled and transported to a site about a mile and a half south of Burlington. On May 24, 1957 the Barrett's new drive-in opened, rechristened as the Burlington Drive-In. They had expanded their old screen, enabling them to top the Malletts Bay Drive-In, advertising the largest screen in the area. By this time the baby boom was in full swing, and the Barretts touted their parent friendly features such as a playground, and a bottle warming service, where an attendant would come to your car, take the bottle, warm it and return it in a matter of minutes. Anything to get people to leave home.

The Burlington Drive-In also opened with a double feature, *Zurak*, and *The Solid Gold Cadillac*. By now it was almost unheard of for drive-ins to offer only one feature film.

Eventually the novelty faded, and the four area drive-ins had to scramble to attract patrons. All of the established indoor movie theaters downtown were still in business, and so the drive-ins started taking out larger, splashier ads for their films, and of course they touted that they offered two movies, while double features were not a regular thing at the indoor theaters. Some weekends a drive-in would offer three, or even four movies. One drive-in started a children under 12 free policy, and the rest soon followed. To combat complaints about sound quality on the old metal speakers that you hung on your car window, drive-ins introduced technology where you could hear the movie dialog over your car's radio. But the visual quality of an outdoor movie could never quite measure up to the indoor screen. Compounding their situation was the word that suburban shopping centers were negotiating to add numerous additional movie screens to those already in operation in Burlington.

By the late 60s drive-in owners were faced with a choice: whether or not to start to show X-rated fare to survive by enticing in an entirely new clientele. The Malletts Bay Drive-In was the first to go that route. In July of 1969 they screened their last conventional movie and started offering X-rated double features. It started paying off almost immediately. Gordon Jarvis, who owned the Malletts Bay Drive-In, reported that his receipts there were three times what he was taking in at the Burlington Drive-In, which he also owned by then. Crowds of 500 cars were not unusual during the summer. He did indicate that his concession sales had dropped though, as those attending his new risqué features "tended to stay in their cars." Unlike the somewhat secluded Malletts Bay, the Burlington Drive-In's screen was viewable from a busy road. Parent Teacher Organizations and others pressured the drive-in owners to make sure that X-rated fare would not be shown on screens easily seen from the road. But soon the Burlington Drive-In would start to show double features that went right up to the X-rated line, but did not cross it. However, they did make an occasional foray into screening X-rated material.

The Mountain View, which had a screen that did not face the road, immediately took the opposite stand, stating that they would only offer family fare, and never X-rated movies.

The Malletts Bay Drive-In would continue to serve up X-rated movies until it closed. When they switched from the old style speakers to the radio method, it created problems. Area residents from Blakely Road to Captain Malletts Steak House complained about the dialog coming into their radios at home, complete with "grunting and groaning."

Gradually the local drive-ins faded from the scene. The Mountain View was gone by 1986, and the Burlington Drive-In closed not long after that. The Malletts Bay Drive-In disappeared from the scene after the summer of 1991. They featured their X-rated double bills right up to the end, showing them for 22 years, longer than they screened traditional movies in their earlier years. So it's no surprise that anyone that remembers these old drive-ins always associates the Malletts Bay with skin flicks.

Image courtesy of the Theatre Historical Society of America.

The roadside marquee of the Burlington Drive-in at 2020 Shelburne Road in 1991, a few years after it closed.

The Suburban Cinemas

As I mentioned in the introduction to this section, downtown Burlington was the only place to see a movie in Burlington from the silent era until the coming of the drive-ins in the late 40s. But Burlington's monopoly on indoor movies lasted until 1970 when Sonderling Broadcasting of Boston constructed Cinema 1&2 in another new shopping center that was being built on Shelburne Road. The cinemas were located between a Martin's supermarket and a Mammoth Mart discount department store (Kmart would soon replace Mammoth Mart).

Cinema 1&2 was a real change for area movie goers, who had long attended films at one of the four downtown theaters, the Majestic, the State, the Strong and the Flynn. The Strong and the Flynn were the closest things that Burlington had to a movie palace. They were large, ornate, with huge screens, a large lobby and a balcony (the Strong had two balconies). The State and the Majestic were more modest. But all four were several cuts above the theaters at Cinema 1&2, which were bare bones, basically a ticket counter and concession stand, a small auditorium with a much smaller seating capacity and a screen smaller than even the most modest of the old Burlington theaters. The new theaters were non-descript in every way, no marquee, just a bland shopping center storefront. Unlike the downtown theaters, the new ones had a sameness about them. But the new cinemas were not without advantages. Their smaller screen was negated by the fact that their much smaller auditorium meant that no seat was very far from the screen. Their seats were more comfortable, and the sound was better. But the chief advantage they had was easy access. Cinema 1&2 and the suburban theaters that would soon follow were located on main throughfares, near interstate exits. They had acres of free parking, so it was easy to park a short walk from the theater.

Moviegoers quickly voted with their feet, and attendance at downtown theaters started to decline. A second twin cinema, Carroll's Plaza 1&2 opened in 1971 on Dorset Street, right off the Interstate 89 cloverleaf. By 1973 a third twin cinema, Showcase 1&2 opened on Williston Road, a short drive east of the cloverleaf exit. In 1974 two more cinemas opened in the A&P shopping center in Essex Junction.

The Strong Theatre was destroyed in a fire in 1971. The Majestic had been demolished in 1956. So that left the Flynn and the State, both of which opened in 1930, to contend with these new suburban cinemas. By 1974 the Flynn had taken the plunge into showing X-rated movies in a desperate attempt to compete with the newcomers. The State Theatre would soon follow suit. In 1977 the State was lost in an explosion and fire. The Flynn soldiered on alone, adding closed circuit events such as boxing matches to its slate of attractions. It also occasionally showed X-rated films. But more and more live events replaced movies, including the debut of a new Burlington community theatre company. Lyric Theatre's first show, *How to Succeed in Business Without Really Trying*, opened at the Flynn in May of 1974. Lyric

The 1980 photo is courtesy of Jerry Chase.

Cinema 1&2 opened in 1970, and was the first of the suburban twin cinemas in the area. It was located next to Martin's supermarket, on the north end of what would come to be known as Kmart Plaza.

would spearhead a drive to acquire the Flynn and refurbish it as a venue for live events. It would be renamed the Flynn Theater for the Performing Arts after a newly formed non-profit purchased it in July of 1981. With that the last of the downtown movie houses faded from the scene, leaving the field entirely to the suburban newcomers.

They would expand, adding screens, and a half price second-run theater named Ethan Allen Cinemas opened behind the North Avenue Shopping Center. But eventually all of those revolutionary suburban cineplexes would close, replaced by the new megaplexes, which opened in even newer shopping complexes and featured nine or ten screens. But Burlington would not be without an indoor movie venue for long, as in December of 1981 the new Nickelodeon Cinemas (now the Roxy) opened a five screen cineplex on the site of an old Shell station on the corner of College Street and South Winooski Avenue.

Photo from the Fred G. Hill Collection/UVM Silver Special Collections.

A crowd waits to enter at the grand opening of Carrol's Plaza 1&2 in 1971. This was the second suburban cinema to open. It was located on Dorset Street in South Burlington, where Barnes and Noble is now.

Bowling

Bowling was a very important part of the Burlington scene for many years. It was a natural for a cold weather city like Burlington. It provided winter entertainment, exercise, socialization, and competition if you wanted it. It was also unusual in that it was a very popular sport for women as well as men.

In the early 20th century, there were only a few bowling locations with a couple of alleys apiece. The earliest bowling alley I found was at the UVM gymnasium when it opened in 1901, but that was not open to the public. The Burlington Bowling Academy opened in 1903 where the Flynn Theater is now. It featured candle pins and was the site of games in the "state league", which featured several Burlington teams.

The earliest Burlington bowling league was the Knights of Columbus league, which started in 1918. They bowled at the Cathedral Alleys. When Cathedral High School opened in 1917 there were two bowling alleys and three pool tables in the basement. As the popularity of bowling grew, more alleys opened and more leagues formed. By 1940 there were five public bowling alleys with nearly 50 lanes in Chittenden County, all in Burlington. In addition there were bowling alleys at several private clubs such as the Ethan Allen Club and the Eagles.

After a lull created by the war, bowling, like many activities covered in this book, exploded out into the suburbs.

Just about all of the pre-war lanes were duck pins. There may have been a few candle pin lanes, but duck pins were by far the most popular form of bowling back then. Leagues tended to be sponsored by social organizations like the Elks, YMCA, K of C or the Daughters of Isabella. Teams were often made up of co-workers.

World War II took a substantial bite out of the bowling community. But when the vets returned after the war, bowling really entered its golden age.

The Greatest Generation was also the last generation of great joiners, and one of the things they joined was bowling leagues. But in addition to the men's leagues, there were high school leagues, ladies' leagues, and afternoon leagues. Hundreds of bowlers competed in leagues, and many more just bowled for the fun of it. The Free Press and Daily News each had a lengthy bowling column that appeared weekly with all the latest bowling news. League standings and scores were a staple of the sports pages.

Although the first two ten pin lanes appeared in Burlington in 1948, duck pins continued to dominate after the war. But the 50s brought big changes. Like retail, bowling started to migrate from the downtown area to the suburbs. That wasn't the only change. As televised bowling matches became more popular, people began to prefer the ten pins that they saw the pros knocking down versus the duck pins that they were accustomed to. So as duck pin lanes closed downtown, they were replaced by ten pin lanes in the suburbs.

Eventually even the ten pin lanes faced their days of reckoning as people moved away from bowling altogether. Ethan Allen Lanes closed in 2000 and the Essex Lanes ceased operations in 2006. Champlain Lanes closed in January of 2019, leaving Spare Time in Colchester as the only bowling alley left in the area.

Bowling had its own unique culture: loud bowling shirts, bowling shoes in crazy colors, having your personal ball that you brought to the alley in a special bag. The sounds of the pins falling, pin boys, and bowling banquets.

The Burlington Bowling Arena

There's no question that when the history of bowling in Burlington is discussed, this is the bowling alley that most people mention first. It was located in the basement of the A&P supermarket on Pearl Street, across from where the federal building is now. It opened in 1938 and lasted until the early 80s. So at this writing there are still many people around who bowled there, or whose fathers and mothers bowled there.

The basement arena had 8 lanes when it opened, but it soon expanded to 12 lanes. Murals of Vermont scenes decorated the side walls. It was strictly duck pin bowling at the Burlington Bowling Arena for most of its existence. The much smaller ball and small pins used in duck pin bowling make it much more difficult than ten pin bowling.

Danny Wilson was the manager from the time the arena opened. He was a native of Scotland and a great golfer. He split his time, managing the bowling arena during the winter. In the summer he was a golf pro, first at the Burlington Country Club for ten years, and then for 34 years at Basin Harbor. He was a golf pro and ran the bowling arena until right before his death in 1974.

As ten pin bowling became more and more popular in area bowling alleys, the Burlington Bowling Arena remained the lone duck pin holdout. Long after the A&P closed the bowling alley hung on. There was a hard core of duck pin bowlers left in town. They sneered at ten pins as being too easy. With that gigantic ball it was easy to score 200 in ten pins, they said. Bowling 200 in duck pins was nearly unheard of. A perfect 300 game has never been bowled in duck pins, while tens of thousands of 300 games are recorded annually in ten pins. The highest score ever recorded anywhere in duck pin bowling was 279. So it was harder, a lot harder, than ten pins. One local bowling alley gave a trophy to anyone who rolled a 150 game. But maybe that's part of the reason duck pins were supplanted by the game with the bigger ball—it was easier to score big.

Finally the population of duck pin devotees dwindled to where the

Photo from the James Detore Archive /UVM Silver Special Collections.

The Burlington Bowling Arena, longtime favorite with area duck pin bowlers is seen in its original eight lane configuration. Located under the A&P on Pearl Street, the Arena was the last duck pin alley to close.

Burlington Bowling Arena was forced to close in the early 80s, but not before establishing itself as a Burlington institution.

Regal Bowling Alleys/Burlington Bowling Center

The Regal Bowling Alleys opened on March 12, 1927 on the second floor of an old livery stable at 163 Church Street. With six alleys it boasted the most up to date equipment in the state. Less than a year after opening, the owner, a man named Michael Baig, decided that he wanted to return to his native New Brunswick, and he sold the Regal Alleys to Alfred Perrotta.

Perrotta is one of the most interesting characters in the history of the Burlington area. He was born in Italy in 1875, came to America in 1886 and moved to Burlington in 1895. He was remarkably active in business. His exploits are far too extensive to detail here, but to summarize, he worked as a foreman for the Rutland Railroad, ran two fruit stores, a movie theater, and was active in construction, contracting, stone quarrying, and especially real estate. Two streets that he developed in Burlington are named for him, Perrotta Place and Alfred Street.

When he was 26 he returned to his home town of Paolisi in Italy, married a local woman there, and returned to Burlington, where they welcomed six children into their family. When his first wife died in 1920, he went back to Italy and married his sister-in-law, who was a widow. She had four children, so the Perrotta home on Perrotta place was a full house.

Perrotta was a lifetime bowler. He was on a team in the first league in Burlington, the Knights of Columbus, when it started in 1919, and remained an active member until right before his death at age 94. He attributed his long life to bowling and "not worrying." After he retired he bowled three times weekly.

Getting back to the Regal Lanes, Perrotta sold the lanes and bought them back again two times between 1928 and 1940. After acquiring them for the third time in 1940, he changed the name to the Burlington Bowling Center. The manager was Perrotta's son Eddie.

The second floor alleys continued to be a popular choice for leagues and for unaffiliated bowlers for about 20 more years. By the early 60s there were many new bowling alleys competing with the Perrotta establishment, and the building was sold. New owner Jack Dubrul ran a speed shop for his racing team on the ground floor. The old bowling alleys on the second floor were removed and the space soon became the home of the Red Dog, a popular Burlington bar for many years.

Photo from the James Detore Archive/UVM Silver Special Collections.

The photo shows the six lane Burlington Bowling Center, an upstairs bowling alley on Lower Church Street. It's all women in the photo, including the painting on the wall. Ads for longtime Burlington businesses are posted above the lanes. From left to right: Mazel's, American Auto Body Paint, Lash Furniture, Endicott Johnson Shoes, White's Dairy, Vermont Paint and Burlington Shoe repairing. The image gives a good comparison of duck pin balls versus ten pin balls.

Ethan Allen Lanes

Developer Tony Pomerleau and builders Bill and Roland Hauke followed up on their Ethan Allen Shopping Center on North Avenue by building a bowling alley in a new structure behind the shopping center. When the Ethan Allen Bowling Center opened in 1955, its 18 lanes made it the largest bowling alley in Chittenden County. Twelve lanes featured the longstanding favorite duck pins, while six lanes were for ten pin bowlers. The duck pin lanes had automatic pin setters, while the ten pin lanes still used pin boys. Tony Pomerleau sold the business to Jack Van Vorst of Utica, NY, who moved to Burlington. The Haukes retained ownership of the building itself. Veteran local bowler Richard Corey was hired to manage the business, and Art Merola was the assistant manager.

This was still the heyday of bowling, and the new lanes had no problem signing up leagues, as well as enjoying a healthy patronage by individual bowlers. Within a year the number of lanes had increased to 24, and they were all automatic. No more pin boys at the Ethan Allen Bowling Center. In 1966 the building was sold to a man named Herman Warner. A brief article about the sale indicated that there were at that point 30 lanes, but I could not verify that. In 1968 two Vermont Air National Guard pilots, Jan Rozendaal and Richard Corley (not Corey) purchased the Ethan Allen Bowling Center, which was also commonly referred to as the Ethan Allen Lanes. Under their corporate name of Airborne Enterprises, the two owned the Williston Road Dilly Wagon and the Sugar House at the Hotel Vermont. They would open a second Dilly Wagon in their North Avenue building.

The prosperity of the Ethan Allen Lanes continued for quite a few years. In 1969 there were no fewer than 17 different leagues bowling there during the winter. But gradually, as the "Greatest Generation" began to pass from the scene, things began to change. As the World War II generation aged, many opted to spend the winter in Florida rather than toughing it out in Vermont and doing things like bowling in a winter league. Winter was the peak season for local bowling. Also, many of the fraternal organizations and businesses that had sponsored bowling leagues and teams either began to struggle or disappeared entirely. The following generation, the Baby Boomers were far less inclined to be "joiners" than their parents' generation, and that included bowling leagues. All of this had a drastic effect on area bowling establishments. The first to close were the small downtown alleys. With the exception of the Burlington Bowling Arena, these were all gone by the early 60s, driven out of business largely by the competition from the larger, newer, suburban bowling centers. But eventually the generational shift just described began to take its toll on those large suburban bowling alleys as well.

The Ethan Allen Bowling Center was the first of these newer bowling venues to close. By the time it announced that it would close in 2000, it was 45 years old, and the oldest of the "new" bowling alleys. On September

21, 2000 the owners threw the alleys open to the public, inviting anyone who wanted to come in and take away for free anything that was literally not nailed down. People grabbed chairs, tables, bowling balls and pins, even ceiling tiles and carpeting. Others just watched as work crews ripped up the shiny hard maple bowling alleys themselves and the pin setting equipment. Those items were destined for the 13 other bowling centers that Richard Corley owned under the corporate mantle of "Bowl New England.

Photo courtesy of Janie Merola McKenzie/Louie Merola Collection.

The Ethan Allen Lanes, behind the Ethan Allen Shopping Center on North Avenue. At 24 alleys, they were the largest bowling center ever in Chittenden County.

Roller Skating / Teen Clubs

Roller skating fans had indoor options in Chittenden County from the 20s until 2017. There were four major venues, one in Burlington, two in Malletts Bay, and one in Williston/Essex. When the final version of Skateland shut down, it left the area without a place to roller skate for the first time in nearly a century.

As mentioned previously, Burlington business leaders responded to a nation wide roller skating craze in the mid 1880s by building a large roller skating rink on the corner of College Street and South Winooski Avenue. The craze soon died out, and the rink was rented out to a furniture dealer. When he left in 1894, the old rink was taken over by the National Guard as their armory, and roller skaters returned to the rink, but roller skating was no longer the primary use of that building. That resource for skaters only lasted until 1903 when the rink burned. When the National Guard opened their new armory building on Pine and Main in 1905, that space became available for roller skaters four nights per week. But the place was still an armory first, available for skating only when not in use by the National Guard. Skaters lost even that when the National Guard armory building became a car dealership. So by the 20s there was no indoor roller skating facility in the area. But that would change by 1928.

The Ethan Allen Pavilion

The Ethan Allen Pavilion was built in 1922 by Ray Beaulieu as a dance pavilion. It was located across from the entrance to Ethan Allen Park, and there was a trolley stop there, so getting to and from the place was relatively easy, at least for that time. The pavilion underwent a management change in 1928, and from that time forward the former dance pavilion started featuring roller skating every afternoon and evening, except for occasional dances. It would be open as a roller skating rink until it ceased operations in 1963.

At some point the Pavilion stopped featuring dances and became exclusively a roller rink. It was winterized in the mid 50s, and open year round. Ray Beaulieu also built the Ethan Allen Cabins, a tourist camp behind the pavilion, but he sold those in 1932. In one of the few existing photos of the pavilion, Texaco gas pumps are seen in front, and those were there due to the tourist cabins in the rear.

Ray Beaulieu sold the Ethan Allen Pavilion in 1946, but kept it in the family, selling to his brother Raoul. He owned it from then until it closed in 1963. In 1965 the old roller rink was demolished and a gas station was erected on the site. Raoul Beaulieu died a couple of months before his old skating rink was torn down.

Photo courtesy of Janie Merola McKenzie/Louie Merola Collection.

The Ethan Allen Pavilion, located near the entrance to Ethan Allen Park. Built originally as a dance pavilion, it later was a roller skating rink for many years as tastes changed. The Texaco gas pumps seen in the front were for the Ethan Allen tourist cabins in the back, which were owned by the proprietors of the roller rink. It was replaced by a Citgo gas station.

Bayside Rollerway

I already covered Clarey's Bayside in the tourist camp section, but their roller skating rink deserves to be singled out here. Like the Ethan Allen Pavilion, the Bayside Rollerway started as a dance pavilion when George Clarey opened his Bayside Pavilion in 1925. People flocked to his pavilion to dance to the music of local, regional, and nationally known bands for decades. But when there was no dance, the huge pavilion with its hardwood dance floor sat empty.

Clarey finally followed the lead of his competitor in Burlington and starting in 1938 he opened Bayside Pavilion to roller skating when there was no dance scheduled, which was most days. He took roller skating to the next level, offering free lessons, free flat shoes to any lady wearing high heels (so she could strap on skates), and special events such as roller skating races and polo on roller skates. A Rollerway Club was formed, with special privileges to members. He held beginners nights, with additional instructors on hand to help the uninitiated get into the sport.

Photo from the James Detore Collection/UVM Silver Special Collections.

Clarey's Bayside in 1957, just a few years before it burned to the ground. Three large overhead doors have been installed across the front to allow light in and so they could be opened up during nice weather. The cabin business has been de-emphasized, and new signage for their arcade and balloons and novelties can be seen.

Bayside boasted the largest skating surface in the state at 10,000 square feet. The hardwood floor was replaced every few years. The Rollerway was seasonal, not operating during the cold months. Getting there was made easy by special buses that ran to Bayside from the Van Ness Hotel in Burlington, and there was even a bus from the Champlain Islands. Taxis also offered special rates to Bayside and back.

Wartime restrictions brought a reduced skating schedule, which at its most restrictive point limited skating to Sundays. But as time progressed things were relaxed and by 1945 roller skating was available Wednesday through Sunday. Roller skating at Bayside was offered every year from 1938 until 1964 when Clarey's Bayside was destroyed in a huge fire in the early morning hours of Saturday, August 8, 1964. The Bayside

Rollerway and the Ethan Allen Pavilion simultaneously offered fun for local skaters for 25 years, and both were gone within a few months of each other.

Photo from the James Detore Archive/UVM Silver Special Collections.

The 10,000 square foot roller skating floor at Clarey's Bayside, by far the largest in the state, is seen in this 1957 photo.

Broadacres

In 1960 Harold Kalf opened an 18 hole miniature golf course in Mallett's Bay on land just to the left of the current Mazza's Grocery store. Miniature golf was in the middle of a nationwide boom. Kalf incorporated as Broadacres Recreation, and the golf course was just the beginning. The following year he added another 18 holes to the course, ten trampolines, and a large go kart track built into a natural basin on the hillside property.

Clarey's Bayside was in the final years of their very long run at this point, and Broadacres was positioning itself to be its successor as the spot for summer recreation at "the Bay." Tastes had changed, and Broadacres, unlike Clarey's had no waterfront. But the land based activities that Kalf offered continued to expand, and people responded.

He added kiddie rides and a picnic area next, and eventually baseball batting cages.

In 1974, in a true echo of Bayside, Broadacres opened a large indoor roller skating rink. The rink also featured an arcade with pinball machines and eventually video games. Clarey's also had an arcade, although I've never seen anyone mention it in the many reminiscences that people have posted on Facebook about Bayside. The new rink enabled Broadacres to become a year round attraction.

I don't have a precise chronology of the decline of Broadacres, but the rising cost of liability insurance played a huge role in the closure of some of its main attractions. That was the reason for the disappearance of the trampolines, the go karts, and eventually the roller skating. The miniature golf hung on for a long time, even as the course became neglected and shopworn. It was still operating in the late 80s.

In 1985 Broadacres stopped offering roller skating due to the high cost of liability insurance. They converted the rink to a teen center. When that didn't go, they re-opened for skating without insurance.

BROADACRES RECREATION

The skating floor at Broadacres, showing the mushroom stools for resting. The party area is in the rear. Author's collection.

Skating continued for a few more years, but eventually the rink became a bingo hall. But the bingo hall was just a vestige of the amazing array of attractions once offered at Broadacres in Mallett's Bay.

There sure was a lot to do in the Burlington area in the 60s.

Skateland

Skateland opened in 1975 on Route 2A in Williston, just north of Taft Corners. It was located in a former motorcycle dealership, Taftway Honda, and featured a 6,000 square foot hard maple skating surface, along with a snack bar. When Skateland opened in April, Chittenden County residents once more had two roller skating options.

In 1977 the large wooden building housing Skateland was completely destroyed in a fire that investigators deemed suspicious. The Burlington area had been enduring an arson epidemic for a number of years, and the loss of Skateland was likely another victim of whoever was setting these fires in the 70s. But this fire is far less remembered than many of the spectacular fires in Burlington during that decade.

Skateland owner Keith Wright vowed to rebuild. True to his word, he contracted with Adams Construction to put up a large steel building as the new home of Skateland, which opened in April of 1979. Now called Skateland Roll-A-Rinx, the new place opened just in time for a fad that was sweeping the country, roller disco. Skaters combined skating with disco moves, often wearing flashy disco themed skates with shiny laces. Disco tunes blared from the sound system, including several written specifically for roller disco. Both Skateland and Broadacres fully embraced the fad while it lasted.

But even as disco and roller disco left the scene, good old fashioned roller skating continued, and many favored Skateland's wood floor over the epoxy over asphalt floor at Broadacres.

Skateland was a popular venue for private events. You could rent the entire place for a private skating or dancing event. It was a very popular place for kids' birthday parties. Parents rented space in the snack bar area for the cake and presents and then party attendees could roller skate. When we lived in Williston we had a birthday party for one of our sons at Skateland. The party guests had just started the skating portion of the party when a skater fell and broke her leg. By the time EMTs arrived and took her away, the time allotted for our skating was over. Murphy's Law was in full effect that day.

By early 2000 Skateland owner Keith Wright had died. His heirs were faced with large estate tax bills, and were forced to sell Skateland to pay them. So Skateland closed on December 30, 2000.

In 2014, after a 13 year hiatus, Skateland was revived, this time in Essex, just west of the Lowe's store off Susie Wilson Road. But this version of Skateland, called Skateland Vermont, had a much shorter run than its Williston predecessor. It closed on May 1, 2017.

Author's collection.

The metal Skateland building in Williston, which replaced the wooden one that burned.

The Teen Clubs

Three teen clubs sprang up in the Burlington area in the mid 60s. These were clubs designed to attract teenagers who needed a place where they could go to enjoy live rock music and dance. The clubs' target audience was kids under the drinking age, so between 14 and 20.

The earliest effort, the Like Young Club, opened in a former Grange Hall on Williston Road in February of 1965. The Grange building was at 1186 Williston Road, and was set way back from the road, almost directly beyond the popular hangout, the Lure. The manager was a man named Rob Roy of Winooski. He had his finger on the teenage pulse, also managing popular local bands like the Vistas, the VaDells, and the Defenders.

But the Like Young concept did not sit well with many parents of teenagers. There is a big difference between a 14 year old and a 20 year old, and fears of young kids being in the same club as kids nearing the drinking age caused a lot of concern. An incident where several 18 year olds were involved in assaults at Like Young confirmed many parental fears. The club space was available for private events on nights when the Like Young Club was closed, which was most nights, as it was not open on school nights. Renting the space out for a "Go Go Beer Blast" probably did not help their credibility with dubious parents of teens. So by the middle of 1967 the Like Young Club was gone.

In January of 1967 another club, Take Over, commonly referred to as the Take Over Club, had opened for business at 117 St. Paul Street. The venture was the brainchild of two well known locals, Jack Hamelle of Shepard and Hamelle, and a future local TV personality Robert "Yancy" Stillinger. They had surveyed area young people and found that they wanted "A place to get together, to listen, or dance to live rock and roll by favorite bands. A place to down soft drinks and snacks, a place to find wholesome entertainment, something to do." As with Like Young, the target clientele was pre-drinking age kids. The goal was to hit the sweet spot between being too square and too "far out." The Take Over was to be a non-profit, with any proceeds going back to the teen community in the form of scholarships and the like.

The Take Over Club was located on the second floor of the old Elks Club building. The space was said to be engineered for "total sound," and fire safety, always a concern in a venue not on the ground floor. The rules of the club, in addition to age restrictions, included no alcohol of course, respect for property and other people, and good taste in dress. Stillinger said that the name Take Over embodied the sponsors' faith in the great majority of kids who suffered due to the misdeeds of a few. He said that someone needed to take over and reach out with a positive approach to give that majority what they wanted and needed.

But the Take Over experiment was short lived. By October of 1967 Stillinger was petitioning the Liquor Control Board for a liquor license, stating his intention to convert the club from an under 21 teen center to an over 21 "young people's dance hall." That request was tabled, and that was the last that was ever heard of the Take Over.

Meanwhile, back at the old Grange Hall at 1186 Williston Road, another effort was underway to launch a teen club right after the closing of the Like

Young Club. This one had the power of a national franchise behind it.

That franchise was based on the NBC television show called Hullabaloo. It aired in prime time in 1965 and 1966 and featured top music acts of the day such as the Rolling Stones, Petula Clark, the Supremes, Lesley Gore, etc. The show was very popular with teenagers, and someone came up with the idea of selling franchises for teen clubs based on the Hullabaloo concept.

Enter Arthur K. Strahan of Greenfield, Massachusetts. He had acquired two Hullabaloo franchises in Vermont, and the Barre location was up and running by the time he approached South Burlington with his proposal for one in the old Grange Hall. He hired Rob Roy, former Like Young Club manager, to manage the new Hullabaloo Club. Although just about everyone referred to it as the Hullabaloo Club, the legal name was the Hullabaloo Scene. It used the logo of the Hullabaloo TV show in advertisements and signage, and every franchisee was required to enforce a strict code of conduct.

Only persons 14 to 20 years of age would be admitted, the club would only be open from 8:00 to 11:30, and then only on nights where there was no school the next day. Strahan explained that there was a strict ban on alcohol, and "hanky panky." There was also no readmittance allowed. Once you left Hullabaloo, you could not get back in that night, even if you offered to pay again. Anyone caught inside with alcohol would be banned for life, and there was no sitting in cars in the parking lot allowed. Deputy sheriffs were hired to patrol the grounds. Parents could enter the club for a four minute look around, but had to leave after that to allow the kids to enjoy the club parent-free.

Impressed by all of this, the South Burlington zoning board granted Hullabaloo a permit to operate, subject to future review. They even granted a variance for Hullabaloo's sign, which was three times the size limit. The 60 foot square sign was erected on Williston Road, right next to the Lure's sign. The Hullabaloo Club was off to a good start.

On Thursday, August 10, 1967, Hullabaloo held an open house for parents. The following night the club opened. The Breakers, a rock group from New York City, was the featured band that night. Also featured were the Hullabaloo Swingers, dancers from the TV show, who appeared at the opening of each franchise.

The Hullabaloo Club proved to be very popular with teenagers. By 1968

Photo courtesy of Rich Crabtree.

The stage at the Hullabaloo Club in South Burlington. The equipment belonged to the Demensions, the house band of Hullabaloo. Their original name was the Dimensions, but when an order of business cards came back with their name misspelled, they just went with the misspelling as their new name.

the average weekend turnout was 1,000 paid customers. But things fell apart relatively quickly. In an underage drinking case, the State's Attorney Patrick Leahy stated that the 18 year old violator had been picked up at the Hullabaloo Club parking lot, "where it seems to be the custom for teenagers to go to drink." This quote brought strong objections from Hullabaloo management. Leahy did clarify his statement, indicating that he did not mean to allege that drinking was occurring inside the Hullabaloo Club. But he went on to explain that Hullabaloo was one of several clubs where they had had trouble with juveniles drinking in the parking lots. The commingling of people in the parking lots at the Lure and Hullabaloo was another problem he stated. He stressed that neither business condoned underage drinking, and had hired deputies to patrol their lots. But these remarks would do nothing to allay the fears of parents about the wisdom of allowing their kids to go to the Hullabaloo Club.

In April of 1968 a request by Rob Roy to operate a recreation center in the basement of Hullabaloo had been unanimously denied by the South

Burlington Selectmen. A request for a renewal of Hullabaloo's permit to operate a dance hall for 1969-70 appears to have been approved. It's not clear when the Hullabaloo Club closed, but South Burlington city records reflect that the building was sold and the club closed by May of 1970.

Resorts

Marble Island Resort

The roots of the Marble Island resort went back to 1881 when the Wakefield Variegated Marble Company was formed in Malletts Bay. A large marble warehouse called the Wakefield Marble Mill was constructed by the firm, which was used for about 30 years and then abandoned. In 1921 the owner of the property, T.R. Brown, began plans to convert the marble mill into a lakefront hotel. The old marble property was located on a peninsula that juts out into Mallett's Bay called Mallett's Head. The property had 193 acres, with three and a half miles of shoreline, and spectacular views of Mallett's Bay. The mill was located right on the water, and for many years the spot was only accessible by boat.

In addition to the hotel, Brown also put in a nine hole golf course, tennis courts, and ten individual bungalows. The property also featured a dock with boats available for the use of guests. The new club proved very popular due to its great location and the wide variety of activities it offered.

Brown came from a very wealthy family in New Jersey. He first came to Vermont in his youth as a summer camper and fell in love with the area. He returned in 1918 and purchased the nearly 200 acre marble company property. He invested much of his time and money into building the club up into a prestigious summer resort.

Brown loved golf and he was very good at it. He won numerous tournaments and topped the field several times at the annual North-South Amateur held at Pinehurst, North Carolina, a tournament that attracted the top players on the eastern seaboard. Despite all of his wealth and talent, Brown lived an incredibly ill fated life.

In 1922 the first tragedy struck as Brown's young wife Elizabeth died after several years of ill health. Brown found distraction through civic involvement, serving on the boards of several local organizations. He remarried, and in 1930 he and his second wife Mary moved into their beautiful new summer home that Brown had constructed on a high knoll overlooking Malletts Bay.

In the fall of 1930 Brown's yacht, said to be one of the finest on the lake, was destroyed by fire. In December of 1932 their new summer home burned to the ground, having stood for only a little over two years. Many priceless antiques, art objects and other furnishings were consumed in the blaze.

Then, in 1934, things got even worse. His wife Mary died suddenly of a heart attack at age 37. Brown's father had died at Malletts Bay three weeks before.

Not surprisingly, Brown's health began to fail. He retreated from civic life and sold the Lake Champlain Club, although he did continue as the club's manager. He married for a third time, and he and his wife continued to spend their summers at the Lake Champlain Club.

In 1939 Brown's life came to an end in a final, horrific tragedy. He was on the fairway at the club enjoying a round of golf when one of the club's buildings caught fire. He and his golfing partner, Burlington banker Edward Thornton, rushed to help fight the flames. They were about 15 feet from the building when a boiler explosion inside hurled a six foot water tank at them like a missile, killing both men instantly. The tank continued down the fairway, killing an Adams School third grader who was at the club with her parents.

Author's collection.

Two large boats anchored at the Marble Island Resort, seen in the background. Around 1967.

In 1940 the Lake Champlain Club was sold to Mr. & Mrs. J. Winthrop Coffin. They ran it until 1964 when it was purchased by a New York attorney named Brickman who summered in Vermont. He immediately made major changes, revamping the golf course, putting in a large swimming pool, enlarging the dock, and drastically remodeling the former hotel/clubhouse. The land was subdivided, and 40 home sites were planned. Most significantly, he changed the name to the Marble Island Golf and Yacht Club, after a small island located a short distance off from the club.

Brickman sold the club in 1965 to the Baird Foundation, run by David Baird, a financier and philanthropist who contributed heavily to numerous Vermont charitable, medical and educational enterprises. All of the club's profits would be turned over to such organizations. Baird added a large banquet room seating 300, along with other changes.

In the following years there were a dizzying series of transactions involving the club that are far too complex to get into here. Suffice it to say that for nearly 40 years Marble Island was a very popular spot for golfing, swimming, boating, class reunions, wedding receptions, etc. But the owner fell into financial trouble and the property went into foreclosure in 2003. The following year the new owners decided to convert it into residential properties, ending its time as a public resort.

Oakledge Manor/Cliffside Country Club

Oakledge was the name given to the first Vermont estate of Dr. William Seward Webb and his wife Lila. Located in the south end of Burlington, the estate had 245 acres and a mile of shoreline. In 1883-1884 they built a large home and numerous outbuildings on the site. The main house sat where the Oakledge Park picnic shelter is now. But after just a few years there they moved to a much larger estate at Shelburne Farms.

In 1926 a group of local investors led by Thomas Wright, and organized as Oakledge Inc., purchased the property with the intent of developing it into a resort. Among the other investors were the other two eventual Wright partners, E.E. Clarkson, and F.D.Abernethy. The private home needed numerous changes to turn the property into a public accommodation. The main ones being the addition of a new 150 seat dining room, and the construction of six cottages away from the main house. The resort offered every summer recreation imaginable, including golf, which was made possible by an arrangement with the Burlington Country Club. Oakledge Inc. recruited A.P. Beach from the Basin Harbor Club to help manage the new resort. In 1929, the resort, named Oakledge Manor, opened for business.

Only six years later, the resort was sold to Fred C. Hill. Under his ownership Oakledge Manor became a popular dining and dancing spot for locals as well as a destination for tourists. Many receptions, parties, school banquets and dances were held there. A stage was built, and the Burlington Theater Club put on their plays there during the 30s and 40s. Fred Hill's widow, reminiscing after Oakledge Manor was gone, said that in all the years they ran it she only saw two people who weren't happy there. One was Joe Dimaggio. He got upset with her when she couldn't get a steak for him (it was during the war).

In 1953, Fred Hill, now in his sixties, leased Oakledge Manor to the Beach family for eight years. At the end of the lease, in 1961, he sold it to employees of General Electric for $138,000. By then the land included was down to 62 acres. They renamed the resort Cliffside.

The new owner, the General Electric Athletic Association (GEAA) was very active at that time. Over 950 GE employees belonged, and that grew to over 1200 with the purchase of Cliffside. Over 1,000 of them descended

Photo from the James Detore Archive/UVM Silver Special Collections.

A wedding reception at Oakledge Manor is pictured in this 1960 photo.

on Cliffside and gave it a thorough refurbishing, cleaning, sanding, painting, etc. It then started operating as Cliffside Country Club.

A nine hole pitch and putt golf course, driving range, tennis courts, cabins (now 15), dining room, bar, dancing, and water sports were among the recreational activities offered. In 1963 GEAA opened membership in Cliffside to non-GE employees. At one point General Electric rented part of Cliffside for use by some of their white collar workers as office space. Cliffside continued to be a popular spot for wedding receptions, banquets, card parties, fashion shows, and the like.

But by 1970 the owners were looking to sell the Cliffside property. A fire later that year did substantial damage to the guest areas, but the kitchen and dining area were untouched, so the club remained open. The owners worked with a New York developer who wanted to build 600 homes there. This was opposed by the city for several reasons. Eventually the city offered to buy Cliffside for $230,000, but that was far from GEAA's asking price of $400,000. After months of wrangling, the city finally did purchase Cliffside's buildings and 45 acres for use as a public park.

More controversy followed regarding what to do with the buildings on the site. The main house was historic, but much of the property had been allowed to deteriorate.

On July 19, 1971 a Burlington fireman set a match to the floors of the old mansion, which had been soaked with gasoline. In a little over an hour the historic main house had burned to the ground. Nearly all of the other buildings were leveled as well. The burning was controversial because it was kept a secret to avoid a large crowd gathering. Besides members of the Parks and Fire departments, few in the city knew this was about to happen. Cliffside was located in Ward 5, and Ward 5 alderman M. Robert Blanchard (no relation) said that neither he nor the other alderman from the ward knew Cliffside was to be burned. The state talked about charging the city with violations of air quality rules due the failure to obtain permits for the burn, but nothing ever came of it. In 1975 the last outbuildings were bulldozed. The gatehouse was the last building to go, in another controlled burn.

The only visible remnants of the Webb/Oakledge Manor/Cliffside years are six cottage chimneys in the woods and a section of flagstone walkway.

Allenwood

For decades the land that became the Allenwood resort had been the Burlington Poor Farm. When South Burlington split off from Burlington in 1865, the 63 acre poor farm was just south of the new Burlington city limits, meaning that it was in the new town of South Burlington. But Burlington retained the poor farm parcel, paying South Burlington for the property. That changed in 1902 when wealthy New Yorker George H. Allen bought the poor farm property.

Allen was born and raised in Whitehall, NY, so he was very familiar with Lake Champlain. He moved to New York City where he made a fortune as a distiller (Paris & Allen). One of his passions was yachting, and he wanted a lakefront estate in the Burlington area to pursue that passion. He also procured land adjacent to the former poor farm, and both parcels were once part of the Pierson farm. The previous owner had erected a dock and cabins for his guests on the property. Allen started pouring money into improvements. The main log cabin was renovated and expanded, and became the residence of George M. Allen, George's son. Carloads of shrubbery were planted, but no changes were made to the actual landscape as Allen wanted to keep it natural. He renamed the estate "Pinewold" and lived in a large mansion that was later separated from what would become the Allenwood resort.

Allen's yacht Alpha was now close at hand for the yachting season on the lake. Although he only summered in Burlington, Allen became a very involved member of the community, joining the Ethan Allen Club, Algonquin Club, Waubanakee golf club as well as the yacht club. He was very active in various local charities.

After enjoying his lakefront mansion and all that went with it for 20 summers, Allen passed away in 1919, just shy of 79 years old.

In 1922 the original Pierson estate was broken up. Allen's son, George Marshall Allen, inherited the northern portion of the estate, about 40 acres which at this point included the main log cabin and four other cabins. George M. quickly sold his portion (1922) to E.P. Woodbury. Woodbury was an experienced operator of hotels in Burlington (Van Ness). His intention in buying the property was to open a resort hotel on it. He set about the job of converting the property into a rustic summer resort, which he named Allenwood, sometimes referred to as the Allenwood Inn.

Allenwood contained many unique features as purchased. The five cabins were connected by covered walkways, and had 15 bedrooms. The main foyer of the large cabin had room for 100 people. Six large plate glass windows provided lake views from anywhere in the foyer. The foyer and dining room were filled with furniture, tapestries and "bric a brac" imported by George Allen from Japan and China. A Japanese garden featured stone lanterns from Japan, ponds with rustic bridges, and was surrounded by a high wall. An entire Japanese tea house had been brought over and reassembled at the Allen estate. A long sandy swimming beach and many other amenities rounded out the package that Woodbury had purchased, which he said would largely be left as is, retaining the rustic log cabin look. Woodbury indicated that Allenwood would become his summer residence. George H. Allen's widow Charlotte retained the southern portion of the original estate, which had been left to her, including the mansion, where she continued to reside. That portion was known as East O Lake.

But in 1926 Mrs. Allen sold an additional 35 acres south of Allenwood to Woodbury. The sale included the mansion, servants quarters, a redstone

Photo from the James Detore Archive/UVM Silver Special Collections.

The entrance to the Allenwood Resort on Shelburne Road in 1947.

garage, boathouse and the stone landing pier for private yachts. A wooded park with a long winding path through rolling meadows and woods with access to Allenwood from Shelburne Road was included. Last but not least was the water system for the estate, with springs and a reservoir, which was located across Shelburne Road.

In 1944 Thomas Farrell bought Allenwood and continued to operate it as a public resort. The main cabin was destroyed in a 1961 fire. A couple years later Farrell offered the property to the city of South Burlington, whose voters twice turned down bond issues that would have enabled them to buy the Allenwood property. The second bond issue was for $130,000.

In 1999 the contents of the original Allenwood buildings were sold at auction. Many of the pieces of furniture were designed and built by Gustav Stickley, a renowned designer of arts and crafts furniture whose work is highly sought after by collectors. Several of his Allenwood pieces were sold at world record prices, including an exceptionally rare cupboard that had only been seen previously in drawings. It shattered the world record for a piece of Stickley furniture, selling for $275,000.

The former Allenwood resort property continues to be owned by the Farrell family, and has been private property for many years. Until recently the four stone gateposts marking the former entrance to Allenwood could be seen by the side of Shelburne Road as you drove by. Three have been removed, and you really have to look closely to spot the last remaining one.

Racetracks

Auto racetracks are really the epitome of the car culture, and like most things associated with that culture, local race tracks sprang up all over Chittenden County in the decade after World War II. Seven racing ovals and one drag strip came and went, most quickly. Somewhat incredibly, five of the tracks were in the town of Colchester. One was near the Sunset Drive-In, one near Holy Cross Church, one on Williams Road, another near the Essex town line off of Route 2A, and one next to the Mallett's Bay Drive-In on Bay Road.

Mallett's Bay Raceway/Bayview Speedway

The longest lasting of the five Colchester racetracks was the racing oval that was located right next to the Mallett's Bay Drive-In on Bay Road (Route 127). The track was built in 1951 by Walt Barcomb, who ran Malletts Bay Salvage, a large auto salvage yard right next to the new oval. In 1952 Barcomb and Ivanhoe Smith dramatically expanded and improved Barcomb's initial track. The track was widened and more steeply banked. The bleacher capacity was tripled. Smith was a used car dealer in Winooski and he also had an excavating business, so he had a lot of heavy equipment, which was used to rebuild the track. Smith had been a competitor of Barcomb's running his own track called the Colchester Raceway, located on Route 2A about midway between Colchester Village and Essex Junction. But after cooperating with Barcomb on his rebuild, Smith partnered with Barcomb at the Bayview Speedway and closed his own track, after only a little over a year in operation.

The track had several names over its existence. Initially called the Bayview Speedway, once Smith came into partnership with Barcomb it became the Colchester-Bayview Speedway. Smith left the picture in 1954 and the track reverted to Bayview Speedway. By 1957 it was known as Mallett's Bay Raceway, sometimes called Mallett's Bay Speedway. The two names seemed to be used interchangeably. The last season for the track was in 1960.

Whatever it was called, this track was the last of the "Colchester Five" to close. After it closed, it would only be a few years before the most successful racetrack ever in Chittenden County opened.

Photo from the Louie Merola Collection, courtesy of Janie Merola McKenzie/Louie Merola Collection.

Cars race past the flagman in this photo of the Malletts Bay Raceway from the 50s. The screen of the Malletts Bay Drive-in can be seen prominently in the background.

The South Burlington Raceway

In 1950 three investors, Leo C. Kirby of Winooski, Earl B. Greer Jr., of Williston, and James P. McKenzie of South Burlington, filed papers to incorporate for the purpose of operating a racing oval in South Burlington. In September of 1950 they opened their new South Burlington raceway for business. The racetrack was located on Dorset Street, about a quarter mile south of Williston Road. The location is about where the South Burlington municipal complex on Market Street stands as this is being written.

The first card of racing was advertised as taking place on Saturday, September 30, 1950. Additional cards were advertised for each of the following weekends through the end of October. And then... nothing. After their opening race day, followed by about a month of racing, the South Burlington Raceway disappears without a trace, at least from the contemporary newspapers.

The next mention of the South Burlington track was 67 years later, a brief mention in a Burlington Free Press article about early race tracks in Chittenden County. The South Burlington Raceway was a "somewhat obscure" track. An understatement to say the least. What happened to it after all that effort to build it and after its one month in operation remains a mystery all these years later.

Photo from the State of Vermont's Open Geodata Portal

The racing oval of the South Burlington Raceway is still clearly visible in the lower right corner of this 1962 aerial image. The Interstate 89 cloverleaf can be seen under construction in the upper left corner.

Catamount Stadium

Catamount Stadium came to be built primarily through the efforts of six men: Ken Squier, who was Thunder Road track announcer and owner of radio station WDEV, Ray and Reggie Fitzgerald, who were paving contractors, Burlington businessman and race car driver Jack DuBrul, car owner Gordon Fitzgerald, and Milton contractor John Campbell. Milton farmer Kermit Bushey was giving up dairy farming, and the six men bought 40 acres of his former farm that was located about a mile north of Chimney Corners on Route 7. The land was flat and open.

Ground was broken for the track in October of 1964. Given the resources

The large sign at the entrance to Catamount Stadium in Milton. Note the farm buildings still standing in the background. The early 1970s photo is from the Lilian Baker Carlisle Collection/UVM Silver Special Collections.

of the six founders, there was not much need for outside contractors to build the track, which was to be a third of a mile steeply banked oval, certified by NASCAR for stock car racing. The track was situated well back from Route 7, and close to the two lanes of the recently completed leg of Interstate 89. Bleachers seating 8,000 that had been used for Lyndon Johnson's 1965 inauguration were purchased, brought to Milton and installed at the track.

Catamount opened on Friday evening, June 11, 1965. A crowd of 6500 was on hand as master of ceremonies George Cameron of WVMT presided over the opening festivities. Miss Vermont of 1965, Lois Dodge of Grand Isle, was driven around the track in the pace car, a Lincoln convertible provided by Lindy-Allen Mercury of Burlington. The track's ultra modern lighting system turned night into day. When it got down to racing, Canada's Jean-Paul Cabana took the 25 lap feature race, his fifth straight win on the NASCAR circuit. His prize was $300. That first race had a little bit of everything, including a five car pileup. The average speed on that first night of racing was 67 miles per hour.

In the early years it was hard to get racers to come to the new track in Milton, given its far northern location. But over the years the reputation of the track grew, and by the 70s big name drivers such as Richard Petty and Bobby Allison were coming to Catamount to race. But by 1980 the glory years were over. That year Tom Curley and Ken Squier lost $60,000 on Catamount races. As a result, weekly races were no longer a regular feature at the track.

By 1985 GBIC (Greater Burlington Industrial Corp.) had acquired the Catamount Stadium property, with the intention of turning it into an industrial park. Catamount continued as an active racetrack for two more seasons. The final race in its storied history was the New England 300, which was held on Sunday, September 20, 1987. Fittingly, veteran Canadian driver Jean-Paul Cabana, who had won the track's first race in 1965, also won that last race ever held at Catamount.

The asphalt oval was soon torn up, and the site was developed for light industry. A state historic marker by the side of Route 7 marks the spot where the entrance to Catamount used to be.

The Milton Drag Strip

The Milton Speedway, also known as the Milton Drag Strip, opened for drag racing in 1963. The owners of the B&M auto salvage yard paved a quarter mile long strip for racing, and an additional quarter mile beyond that for slowing down.

The Speedway wasn't in business for very many years, but while it was, the top names in drag racing appeared there. "Big Daddy" Don Garlits,

Photo by Henry DeWolf/Milton Historical Society.

An aerial view of the Milton Speedway drag strip.

probably the best known drag racer ever, raced at Milton in 1969. Shirley "Cha Cha" Muldowney competed there early in her career along with her husband Jack. She was the first woman licensed to drag race professionally. Unlike other sports, there is no women's league in racing. Any ladies who wanted to compete did so against the men. In her career she regularly beat the top male racers, winning 18 nationally sanctioned events, and three national championships.

Shirley Muldowney was born in Burlington as Shirley Ann Roque. Her father was Belgium "Tex" Roque, who sidelined as a local country singer. Shirley was still quite young when the family relocated to Schenectady, where she met her husband and mechanic, Jack Muldowney. Ironically, when she married him at 16 years of age, she didn't know how to drive a car. Two years later she started racing. Hollywood made a movie of her life, *Heart Like a Wheel*, starring Bonnie Bedelia and Beau Bridges.

The Milton strip closed in 1970. Its distinctive red and white checkerboard tower later ended up at Catamount Stadium. Decades after it closed the drag strip was still plainly visible when you drove by the former location. A state historic marker now stands on the former speedway site.

Still Here: Enduring Icons

Although the theme of this book is bygone attractions, I felt that I would be remiss if I did not pay homage to several local establishments that have been around for generations and continue to thrive as of this writing. These three restaurants have each been in business in Chittenden County for 70+ years, with one approaching the century mark. Remarkable for any business, but particularly impressive in the notoriously tough restaurant trade. These are truly local icons.

Al's French Frys

In August of 1913 a ship by the name of *Caroline* pulled into harbor in Quebec City. On board were hundreds of immigrants from Europe, most of whose destinations were in Canada. Among the immigrants was Ida Rusterholz from Switzerland, who was on the *Caroline* with her two sons, three year old Adolph Junior, and one year old Albert. They were destined for Vermont. Her husband Adolph had left Switzerland earlier, and had secured a job at the Hood creamery in Morrisville.

The boys grew up in Underhill and Cambridge. The coming of the Depression saw Adolph and the two boys living as boarders in Whiting, Vermont, apparently getting work wherever they could find it. Ida and Elsa, their daughter born after arriving in Vermont, lived elsewhere. More wanderings followed, with home and business addresses for the couple including Bethel, Manchester, Orleans, and Pittsfield.

Eventually young Albert moved to Detroit, but he met a young woman from Essex Junction named Genevieve Smith. Their 1941 wedding announcement indicates that Albert had returned to Vermont and was managing a cheese factory in Essex Junction. But he soon left that job because by the end of 1942 he had taken a lease on an existing dry cleaning business in town, and became the operator of Stanton's Dry Cleaning.

In June of 1943 "Al and Gen" opened their own dry cleaning business, and named it Al's Cleansing Service. It was located at 10 Main Street in the Junction, in the former post office space.

But apparently the couple grew tired of cleaning other people's clothes, and after less than two years in business, they sold the dry cleaning shop. They headed for Detroit to pursue an unspecified business opportunity. When that didn't pan out they headed back to Vermont, and on the drive back they discussed their next business venture.

The Champlain Valley Fair was coming up, and the couple decided to try selling French fries at the fair. They rented a small booth and Albert set up an oil stove and a small pan for frying. So the first time Vermonters tasted Al's French Frys was at the 1945 Champlain Valley Fair. With Al's it has always been frys, not fries. This was Genevieve's idea. She thought it would set them apart from the competition.

Encouraged by their one week of selling at the Essex fairgrounds, they proceeded south to Rutland, and sold their French fries at the Rutland Fair the following week. Success there convinced them that they were on

Photo from alsfrenchfrys.com.

Al's French Frys first stand on Williston Road in South Burlington, which opened in 1950. The neon sign by the side of the road showed a cup of fries with the words "Al's French Frys" on it.

to something. But cold weather was arriving in Vermont, and they were only equipped for outside selling. So they decided to head to Florida and keep at it. Al built his own trailer, equipped with two frying wells heated by bottled gas. A hand operated machine for slicing potatoes into French fries completed the setup.

They headed for Winter Park, a suburb of Orlando, where they met many Vermonters. It's hard to believe, but at that point, Orlando wasn't much bigger than Burlington. They had a street location in Winter Park, and on Sundays they moved the trailer to Seminole Racetrack. They also set up at various festivals, and after the Orlando Fair they headed back to Vermont.

They set up for the summer of 1946 in Malletts Bay at Nourses, a well known snack bar at the bay. From the first day they started, customers could not get enough of their hand cut fries, fresh out of the hot oil.

At the end of the summer they returned to the Champlain Valley Fair, rounding out a busy first year. But they still only had a trailer, and were not equipped to sell at retail in cold weather. So in March of 1947 they launched a frozen version of Al's French Frys in conjunction with the Champlain Valley Fruit Company.

The arrival of warm weather saw Al's with two trailers, one at Nourses, and another on Main Street in Essex Junction, virtually across the street from their old Al's Cleansing Service location. During fair week, both trailers were set up at the fairgrounds, one at either end of the grandstand. This tradition continues to this day, with multiple Al's outlets set up during the now 10 day Champlain Valley Fair.

Finally, in June of 1948, it was announced that Al's first permanent building would be constructed on the Main Street site occupied by their Essex Junction trailer. This meant that you could get your Al's French Frys fix year round, so no more need for the frozen variety. The first sign at the Essex Junction site featured a large statue of a creemee and the sign said "Al's Snack Bar", not "Al's French Frys". The trailer continued to operate during the summer at Malletts Bay.

In May of 1950 Al's expanded, constructing a second stand at their current location on Williston Road. This was the first drive in snack bar to locate in South Burlington. Dozens would follow, some locally owned like Al's, but most were national chains.

Somewhat surprisingly, French fries were not mentioned on the Williston

Road building's signage, only on the sign by the side of the road. The building signage said "Al's Snack Bar", with the words "Frozen Custard" across the roof. A neon sign right on Williston Road did say "Al's French Frys." In April of 1954 an ad for Al's Williston Road location claims to be the home of Vermont's first two flavored frozen custard cone, now known as a twist when you order a creemee.

It was a bit of a surprise to me that the original Al's in Essex Junction continued to operate for many years after Williston Road opened. Somewhere along the way Al and Gen divorced, and in the settlement Gen got sole control of the restaurants. She sold the Essex Junction Al's in 1970.

By the early 80s she was ready to retire, and sold the Williston Road Al's to Bill and Lee Bissonette, two brothers from Burlington with no experience in the restaurant business. But they knew enough not to make any major changes. Gen continued to advise the brothers until her death at 96 in 2001.

Al also remarried after relocating to St. Albans. He died in Florida in 1988 and is buried in Underhill. But nearly 80 years after serving those first fries at the Fair, his name lives on in the hearts and taste buds of locals.

Henry's Diner

The restaurant business is well known for the extremely high failure rate of new ventures. According to CNBC data, 80% of new restaurants close within five years of startup, which makes the longevity of Henry's even more remarkable. I've always used 100 years in business as a benchmark for icon status among area stores, and 50 years for eateries. As this is being written, Henry's Diner is fast approaching its 100th year in business dispensing meals at the same location on Bank Street in Burlington. A truly remarkable achievement.

It was founded in 1925 by Henry Couture, who came to Burlington from Rouses Point, New York determined to open a diner. He faced several obstacles. The churches and the "upper crust" of Burlington opposed having a diner in their town. They were considered "greasy spoons" that attracted rowdies and were a bad influence for children. But after three meetings with the Board of Alderman, Henry got the go ahead, and immediately ordered a diner from a company in Bayonne, New Jersey. The diner Henry ordered was a rarity—it is the only diner made of wood in the area. It was clad in

Author's collection.

Henry's Diner not long after opening in 1925. The center entrance and all of the other original features seen here have long been changed or hidden by a substantial renovation/expansion.

automobile steel on its lower half. It was shipped north by rail and installed on Bank Street in June of 1925. The original signage had "Henry's Diner" on the right of the center entrance door. Henry's was in flowing script, and Diner in block letters. On the left it said "Clean Wholesome Food, Nothing but the Best Served Here." When Henry's opened, the safety of food, and even of water was of great concern to most.

Henry used new marketing strategies such as appealing to women. It was frowned upon back then for women to go to a diner. He put up awnings and flower boxes at the entrance and added menu items he thought would appeal to women such as waffles for breakfast. Once a year he had giveaways of Kewpie dolls and billfolds. It all worked because business steadily increased. Churchmen admitted that they had been wrong about Henry's diner and even society people began to patronize it. The diner was expanded to accommodate booths in 1935, and an air lock entry was installed to protect diners from cold winter blasts.

By 1944 Henry's health forced him to sell. The buyer was Charles Chantis, owner of the Black Cat Café. But for some mysterious reason, three weeks later he sold the diner to Frank and Roberta Goldstein and their business partner Sam Rothman. When they bought it Henry's was open from 6 am to 2 am. Frank started closing the diner earlier because the late closing time was attracting rowdies. Frank was born in Plattsburgh, raised in Burlington, and worked out of state for a number of years before returning here. The Goldsteins also owned the A&W downtown, which was run by their son Michael. A 1969 fire at Henry's was a major setback, but the Goldsteins were able to repair the damage and reopen.

In 1974 the Goldstein's sold the A&W and Michael, who was also a brigadier general in the Vermont National Guard, moved over to manage Henry's. Frank Goldstein died in 1982. On November 25, 1999 the Free Press announced the closing of Henry's. But less than two weeks later, James Flood of Rutland, a diner lover, stepped in and reopened it. For many years it's been owned by Bill Maglaris, whose family history in the Burlington restaurant business goes way back (the Arcadia Restaurant). Henry's remains open, and no other Burlington eating establishment has lasted longer.

Under both Henry Couture and the Goldsteins, the diner was a place where the staff stayed on for decades. There were numerous cases of cooks and waitresses who were there 25 or 30 years or more. Obviously, it was a good place to work.

The Parkway Diner

The Parkway Diner sits at 1696 Williston Road, just a bit west of Airport Drive. The diner has been in the same spot since 1953. But when it first opened it was not called the Parkway, it was known as Farid's Diner. Farid Simon ordered a Worcester Diner, number 839, manufactured by the Worcester Lunch Car and Carriage Manufacturing Company of Worcester, Massachusetts.

Unfortunately, Farid's tenure running his new diner did not last long. Less than two years later the diner was put up for auction at a sheriff's sale. This apparently was the result of some sort of illness.

In October of 1956 the Lines brothers, George, Gus and Bill, opened the newly renamed Parkway Diner. The Lines family's history in the Burlington restaurant business went back to their Burlington Lunch on Church Street (1916), and their Burlington Sweet Shop (1920) at Church and Main.

The Lines family would go on after that to have a hand in running numerous Burlington Restaurants, including other diners: The Oasis, The Majestic, and The Miss Burlington.

By the mid 70s the Parkway had been sold to George Hatgen, an experienced area restauranteur. In 1989 his son Peter took over running the Parkway. By 1997 George and Christine Alvanos were running the diner, leasing it from George Hatgen, who still owned the property. In 2006 the Alvanos bought Red Robert's store with plans to turn it into a deli. So they ended their management of the Parkway in March of 2007. Peter Hatgen, now known as Peter Hatgigiannis, resumed running the diner after the Alvanos left.

The diner itself was now nearly a half century old, and needed some freshening up. A new prep kitchen, new restrooms, and reupholstered stools and booths were among the improvements undertaken at this time, along with a general cleaning from top to bottom. Despite all of this, to the untrained eye the interior looked the same as the day the diner was delivered in 1953. After being closed for several months the Parkway reopened in October of 2007. Like most diners, the Parkway was a favorite breakfast spot. Breakfast is served all day, or I should say as long as they are open. The Parkway only serves breakfast and lunch.

By 2015 Colchester native Corey Gottfried had acquired the diner. He was committed to making as much food from scratch as possible and also maximizing the use of locally produced ingredients. By this time numerous other local restaurants were offering different takes on breakfast, providing options nonexistent in the early days of the Parkway. Could the Parkway

Photo from the Lilian Baker Carlisle Collection/UVM Silver Special Collections.

The Parkway Diner on Williston Road, a Chittenden County perennial for over 70 years.

and two other Chittenden County diners offering similar comfort food make it in the new Burlington breakfast scene?

The answer seemed to be a resounding yes, but then the COVID-19 pandemic changed everything. In June of 2020 the Parkway posted a notice on Facebook announcing the closing of the diner. The wording led many to believe that the Parkway was closing permanently. A clarification quickly was issued, stating that the operators of the Parkway hoped to re-open once conditions improved.

But as the Parkway's closure dragged on, well after other local restaurants had reopened, many feared that they had eaten their last meal at the Parkway. But finally, after being shut down for two years, the Parkway finally reopened under the new management of Brian Lewis.

So happily, at this writing the Parkway is again serving breakfast and lunch, and the appetite for its offerings seems as healthy as ever.

Author Biography

Bob Blanchard was born and raised in the South End of Burlington, Vermont. He was educated in Burlington Catholic schools, and graduated from the University of Vermont with a degree in history. After a 35 year career with the U.S. Customs Service in Vermont and New York, he took up local history as a serious hobby. His Burlington Area History Facebook group has found a large audience for its daily postings. That experience has taught him two main things: that people love historic photographs, and that nostalgia postings get far more reaction than history postings. Bygone Attractions of Chittenden County was written with both of those things in mind.

After having several articles published, he published his first book, Lost Burlington, Vermont, in 2023. He currently resides in St. Albans, Vermont with his wife Linda.

Printed in the USA
CPSIA information can be obtained
at www.ICGtesting.com
LVHW062203080724
784979LV00017B/378